ISBN-13: 978-1951244477
Printed in the United States of America

Foreword

About Myself

For many years I struggled to learn Spanish, and I still knew no more than about twenty words. Consequently, I was extremely frustrated. One day I stumbled upon this method as I was playing around with word combinations. Suddenly, I came to the realization that every language has a certain core group of words that are most commonly used and, simply by learning them, one could gain the ability to engage in quick and easy conversational Spanish.

I discovered which words those were, and I narrowed them down to three hundred and fifty that, once memorized, one could connect and create one's own sentences. The variations were and are *infinite*! By using this incredibly simple technique, I could converse at a proficient level and speak Spanish. Within a week, I astonished my Spanish-speaking friends with my newfound ability. The next semester I registered at my university for a Spanish language course, and I applied the same principles I had learned in that class (grammar, additional vocabulary, future and past tense, etc.) to those three hundred and fifty words I already had memorized, and immediately I felt as if I had grown wings and learned how to fly.

At the end of the semester, we took a class trip to San José, Costa Rica. I was like a fish in water, while the rest of my classmates were floundering and still struggling to converse. Throughout the following months, I again applied the same principle to other languages—French, Portuguese, Italian, and Arabic, all of which I now speak proficiently, thanks to this very simple technique.

This method is by far the fastest way to master quick and easy conversational language skills. There is no other technique that compares to my concept. It is effective, it worked for me, and it will work for you. Be consistent with my program, and you too will succeed the way I and many, many others have.

CONVERSATIONAL ROMANIAN QUICK AND EASY SERIES

The Most Innovative Technique To Learn the Romanian Language

PART - 1, PART – 2, PART - 3

YATIR NITZANY

Check out my website:
www.Conversational-Languages.com

CONTENTS

The Romanian Language

The Romanian language developed from **Latin**, brought to the region of Dacia (modern Romania) by Roman colonists after the Roman conquest in the 2nd century AD. Over time, Vulgar Latin evolved differently in this area, influenced by local Dacian languages, as well as by Slavic, Greek, Hungarian, and Turkish languages. This created a unique Romance language, distinct from other Latin-derived languages like Italian, French, and Spanish.

During the Middle Ages, Romanian was primarily a spoken language, while Church Slavonic was used in written documents. The influence of neighboring Slavic cultures introduced new vocabulary and phonetic changes, shaping the development of early Romanian. Romanian dialects also began to emerge, reflecting regional differences in pronunciation and vocabulary across Wallachia, Moldavia, and Transylvania.

In the 16th to 18th centuries, Romanian started to be written more frequently in the Latin alphabet, replacing the Cyrillic script used in some regions. Literary works, religious texts, and legal documents helped standardize the language, while the influence of Western European languages like French and Italian introduced further vocabulary and stylistic elements.

Today, Romanian is spoken by over 25 million people as a first language, primarily in Romania and Moldova. It remains a Romance language with strong Latin roots, enriched by centuries of cultural interactions and historical changes. Modern Romanian continues to evolve, blending its heritage with contemporary influences while preserving a connection to its unique history in Eastern Europe.

Romanian Pronunciation Guide

a is pronounced similar to the "a" in "rather"

e is pronounced similar to the "a" in "crate"

i is usually pronounced similar to the "ee" in "meet"

o is pronounced similar to the 'o' in "chore"

u is pronounced similar to the 'oo' in "room",

ă is pronounced similar to the 'a' in "aloud"

â and î are both pronounced similar to the "i" in "twirl". However, î only appears at the beginning of the word while â appears everywhere else in the word.

Consonants

ş is pronounced similar to the 'sh' in "rush"

ţ is pronounced similar to the 'ts' in "sports"

c (ce) proceeded by an i or e, is pronounced similar to the 'ch' in "cheer", otherwise like the 'c' in "cry".

ch solely appears preceding i or e, is pronounced similar to the 'c' in "cry".

g (ghe/ge) when followed by i or e, pronounced similar to the 'j' in "jar", otherwise like the 'g' in "goose".

gh solely appears preceding an i or e and is pronounced similar to the 'g' in " goose".

Diphthongs

oi is pronounced similar to the 'oy' in "joy".

ea is pronounced similar to the 'a' in " crate " followed by the 'a' in "rather".

ai is pronounced similar to the 'i' in "ride".

ei is pronounced similar to the 'a' in "lane".

au is pronounced similar to the 'ou' in "south".

ău is pronounced similar to the 'a' in "amount" proceeded by the 'oo' in "loot".

ăi is pronounced similar to the 'a' in " amount " proceeded by the 'ee' in "meet".

âi is pronounced similar to the Romanian 'â' or 'î' proceeded by the 'ee' in "meet".

îi is pronounced similar to the "i" in "like".

Conversational Romanian Quick and Easy

The Most Innovative Technique to Learn the Romanian Language

Part I

YATIR NITZANY

Introduction to the Program

People often dream about learning a foreign language, but usually they never do it. Some feel that they just won't be able to do it while others believe that they don't have the time. Whatever your reason is, it's time to set that aside. With my new method, you will have enough time, and you will not fail. You will actually learn how to speak the fundamentals of the language—fluently in as little as a few days. Of course, you won't speak perfect Romanian at first, but you will certainly gain significant proficiency. For example, if you travel to Romania, you will almost effortlessly be able engage in basic conversational communication with the locals in the present tense and you will no longer be intimidated by culture shock. It's time to relax. Learning a language is a valuable skill that connects people of multiple cultures around the world—and you now have the tools to join them.

How does my method work? I have taken twenty-seven of the most commonly used languages in the world and distilled from them the three hundred and fifty most frequently used words in any language. This process took three years of observation and research, and during that time, I determined which words I felt were most important for this method of basic conversational communication. In that time, I chose these words in such a way that they were structurally interrelated and that, when combined, form sentences. Thus, once you succeed in memorizing these words, you will be able to combine these words and form your own sentences. The words are spread over twenty pages. In fact, there are just nine basic words that will effectively build bridges, enabling you to speak in an understandable manner (please see Building Bridges, page 33). The words will also combine easily in sentences, for example, enabling you to ask simple questions, make basic statements, and obtain a rudimentary understanding of others' communications. Please see Reading and Pronunciation (Page 7) in order to gain proficiency in the reading and pronunciation of the Romanian language prior to starting this program.

My book is mainly intended for basic present tense vocal communication, meaning anyone can easily use it to "get by" linguistically while visiting a foreign country without learning the entire language. With practice, you will be 100 percent understandable to native speakers, which is your aim. One disclaimer: this is *not* a grammar book, though it does address minute and essential grammar rules, so keep your eyes peeled for grammar footnotes at the bottom of every page. Therefore, understanding complex sentences with obscure words in Romanian is beyond the scope of this book.

People who have tried this method have been successful, and by the time you finish this book, you will understand and be understood in basic conversational Romanian. This is the best basis to learn not only the Romanian language but any language. This is an entirely revolutionary, no-fail concept, and your ability to combine the pieces of the "language puzzle" together will come with *great* ease, especially if you use this program prior to beginning a Romanian class.

This is the best program that was ever designed to teach the reader how to become conversational. Other conversational programs will only teach you phrases. But this is the *only* program that will teach you how to create your *own* sentences for the purpose of becoming conversational.

The Program

Let's Begin! "Vocabulary" (Memorize the Vocabulary)

I - Eu
I am - Eu sunt
Are you – Ești/ Sunteți [singular/plural]
He / she - El / ea
With you - Cu tine
With him - Cu el
with her - Cu ea
With us - Cu noi
For you - Pentru tine
Without him - Fără el
Without them - Fără ele/ fāra ei
Home – Acasă/casă
This – Acesta/Aceasta [masc/fem] singular
Is, it's - Este
Always – Întotdeauna/Mereu [synonym]
Was - A fost/Era [synonym]
Sometimes – Uneori /Câteodata [synonym]
From - Din

Are you at the house?
(Tu)Ești/(Voi) Sunteți acasă? [sing/plu]
Sometimes I go without him.
Uneori (eu) plec fără el.
I am always with her.
Eu sunt întotdeauna/mereu cu ea.
I am from Romania.
Eu sunt din Romania.
Are you from Bucharest?
(Tu) Ești/(Voi) Sunteți din București?
I am with you
Eu sunt cu tine/voi [sing/plu]
Are you alone today?
(Tu) Ești singur/singură azi? [masc/fem]
This is for you
Asta/aceasta este pentru tine/voi [fem] [sing/plu]
Ăsta/acesta [masc] este pentru tine.

Good - Bun
Better - Mai bine
Happy - Fericit
I was – Eu am fost
Later - Mai târziu
After - După
Tomorrow - Mâine
And - și
Between - Între
Here - Aici
Now - Acum
If - Dacă
Yes - Da
Then - Apoi
Then - Atunci
Also - De asemenea
Too - Și
As well - La fel
Where - Unde
Ok – Ok, Bine, În regulă
Somewhere - Undeva
Maybe - Poate

Where are you?
Unde esti/sunteți tu/voi? [sing/plu]
I was home at 5pm.
Eu am fost acasă la 5 PM.
Between now and tomorrow.
Între acum și mâine.
It's better to be home later.
Este mai bine să fii acasă mai târziu.
If this is good, then I am happy.
Dacă acest lucru este bun, atunci eu sunt fericit/fericită. [masc/fem]
Yes, you are very good.
Da, (tu) eşti foarte bun/bună. [masc/fem]
I was here with them.
Eu am fost aici cu ei/ele. [masc/fem]
Maybe somewhere.
Poate undeva.

Me - Eu
This is - Acesta/Aceasta este
That is – Acela/Aceea este [masc/fem]
There - Acolo
Even if - Chiar dacă
Everything - Totul
What - Ce
Almost - Aproape
You – Tu
You – (Plural) voi
The - (M) l, ul
The - (M-plural) i
The - (F) a, ua,
The - (F-plural) le
The - (N-singular) l, ul
The - (N-plural) le

You and I.
Tu si eu.
Even if I go now.
Chiar dacă eu merg acum.
Where is everything?
Unde este totul?
What? I am almost there.
Ce? Eu sunt aproape acolo.
This is for us.
Aceasta/Acesta este pentru noi. [fem/masc]
The boy is at school.
Băiat**ul** este la școală.

*In Romanian the definite article is placed at the end of the noun as a suffix.
For example: The masculine noun (singular, nominative/accusative) "boy" / *baiat* and "the boy" is *baiatul* and plural "the boys" *băiții*
"father" / *tată* and "the father" is *tat**ăl**.*
"number" / *număr* and "the number" is *număr**ul***
The feminine noun (singular, nominative/accusative)
"flower" / *floare* and "the flower" / *flore**a**.*
"girl" *fat* and "the girl" *fat**a*** and plural "the girls" / fete**le**
Regarding neuter nouns (singular, nominative/accusative)
"place" / *loc* and "the place" is *loc**ul**.*

Without us - Fără noi
Son - Fiu / **Daughter -** Fiică
Car - Mașină / automobil
House - Casă
Good morning - Bună dimineața
How are you? - Ce mai faci?
Where are you from? - De unde ești/sunteți? [sing/plu]
What is your name? - Cum te numești? / Care este numele tău?
How old are you? - Cîti ani ai?
Today - Azi
Hello – Salut/Bună
Hard – Greu
In - În / **At -** La
Already - Deja
Very - Foarte
A - Un / o (see footnote)

She is without a car, so maybe she is still at the house?
Ea este fără mașină, așa că poate este încă la casă?
I am in the car already with your son and your daughter.
Eu sunt în mașină deja cu fiul și cu fiica ta.
Good morning, how are you today?
Bună dimineața, cum ești/sunteți astăzi? [sing/plu]
Hello, what is your name?
Bună, care este numele tau?
How old are you?
Ce vârstă ai/aveți tu/voi? [sing/plu]
This is very hard, but it's not impossible.
Acest lucru este foarte greu, dar nu este imposibil.
Where are you from?
De unde ești/sunteți? [sing/plu]

*In Romanian the indefinite article is placed at the beginning of the noun. Regarding masculine and neuter:
Un (nominative/accusative) and unui (genitive/dative):
"Friend" / *prieten* and "a child" is *un prieten*
"Place" / *loc* and "a place" is *un loc*
Regarding feminine:
O (nominative/accusative) and unei (genitive/dative):
"Bottle" / *sticlă* and "a bottle" *o sticlă*
"Emergency" / *urgențe* and "an emergency" / *unei urgențe*

Thank you - Mulțumesc
For – Pentru
In order to - Pentru a
Yesterday - Ieri
Time - Timp
Since - De când
Before - Înainte
No / not - Nu
I am not - Eu nu sunt
That – Că, Acea / **That –** Acel
But - Dar
Away - Departe, Plecat
Similar – Similar / **Similar –** La fel
Anything - Orice
Another (a different one in general) **–** (m) Altul, (f) alta
Another (a different one more specific) **–** (m) Celălalt / (f) cealaltă
Another (an additional one) **-** Încă o/Încă oun
Side - Parte
Until - Până
Still - Totuși

Thank you, Kenneth.
Mulțumesc, Kenneth.
It's almost time.
E aproape timpul.
I am not here, I am away.
(Eu) Nu sunt aici, sunt plecat.
That house is similar to ours.
Acea casă este similară cu a noastră.
I am from the other side.
Eu sunt din cealaltă parte.
But I was here until late yesterday.
Dar eu am fost aici până ieri târziu.

*In Romanian there are three ways of expressing "time":
Occasion / instance - **dată / ori**
Prima **dată** - The first **time** / De trei **ori** - Three **times**
Duration / period - **timp**
În **timpul** dinozaurilor - During the **time** of the dinosaurs
Clock / hour **oră**
La ce **oră** începe filmul? - At what **time** does the movie start?

To be - A fi
I say / I am saying - Eu spun
To see - De văzut/A vedea
I see / I am seeing – Eu văd
I want – Eu vreau
I need – (Eu) am nevoie
I go / I am going – Eu plec /Mă duc /Merg
What time is it? - Cât este ceasul?
Without you - Fără tine
Everywhere - Peste tot
With - Cu
My - (Singular) A mea
My - (Plural) Ale mele
Cousin - Văr
Right now – Acum
Night - Noapte
Light - Lumină
Outside - Afară
That is – (m) Acesta
That is – (f) Aceasta este
Any – Oricare/Orice

I am saying no / I say no.
Eu spun că nu/ Eu spun nu.
I want to see this during the day.
(Eu) Vreau să văd asta în timpul zilei.
I see this everywhere.
Eu văd asta peste tot.
I am happy without any of my cousins here.
(Eu) Sunt fericit fără niciunul dintre verii mei aici.
I need to be there at night.
(Eu) trebuie să fiu acolo noaptea.
You need to be at home.
(Tu) Trebuie să fii acasă.
I see light outside.
Eu văd lumină afară.
What time is it right now?
Ce oră este acum?

*This *isn't* a phrase book! The purpose of this book is *solely* to provide you with the tools to create *your own* sentences!

To wait - A aştepta
To sell – A vinde
To sell – De vânzare
To use - A folosi
To know - A şti, A cunoaşte
To decide - A decide, A hotărî
To find - A găsi
To look for / to search - A căuta
To - Pentru
Place - Loc
Easy - Uşor
Near / nearby – Aproape
Between - Între
Both – Ambele
To lift – A ridica

This place is easy to find.
Acest loc este uşor de găsit.
I am saying to wait until tomorrow.
Eu spun să aștept/aşteptăm până mâine. [sing/plu]
It's easy to sell this table.
Este uşor să vinzi acestă masă.
I want to use this.
(Eu) Vreau să folosesc asta.
I need to decide between both places.
(Eu) Trebuie să decid între ambele locuri.
I need to know that everything is ok.
(Eu) Trebuie să știu că totul este în regulă.
I need to look for you at the mall.
(Eu) Trebuie să te caut la mall.
Is this place nearby?
Este acest loc aproape?
I want to lift this.
(Eu) Vreau să ridic asta.

*In the Romanian language, nouns have three genders; masculine, feminine and neuter. Nouns ending in a **consonant** or **-u** are usually masculine or neuter and the plural ending is usually **-i**. Nouns ending in an **-a** or an **ă** are usually feminine and the plural ending is usually **-e** for feminine or neuter. However, there are exceptions!

To look – A se uita
To buy - A cumpăra
To understand - A înțelege
I can - Eu pot
Can I - Pot eu
Myself – însumi/însămi [masc/fem]
Mine - A mea
Them – Lor
They - Ei
Book - Carte
Food - Mâncare
Water - Apa
Hotel - Hotel
Problem / Problems - Problemă / Probleme
Enough - Destul
Because - Pentru că
Like this - (m) Ca acesta /**(f)** Ca aceasta
Like this - (neuter) Așa
Of - De

I like this hotel because it's near the beach.
(Mie) Îmi place acest hotel pentru că este lângă plajă.
I want to look at the view.
(Eu) Vreau să mă uit la priveliște.
I want to buy a bottle of water.
(Eu) Vreau să cumpăr o sticlă cu apă.
Do it like this!
Fă așa!
I want something like this.
Vreau ceva ca acesta.
Both of them have enough food
Amândoi/Amândouă au mâncare suficientă. [masc/fem]
That book is mine.
Cartea aceea e a mea.
I need to understand the problem.
(Eu) Trebuie să înțeleg problema.
I have a view of the city from the hotel.
(Eu) Am o vedere spre oraș de la hotel.
I can work today.
Eu pot lucra astăzi.

To know - A şti
To work - A munci
To say - A spune
To go - A merge
I like - Îmi place
Family - Familie
Parents Părinţi
There is - Există
There are - Sunt
Who - Cine
Why – De ce
Something - Ceva
Ready - Gata
Soon - Curand
I do / I am doing - Eu fac
Hospital - Spital

I like to be at my house with my parents.
(Mie) Îmi place să fiu acasă cu părinţii mei.
Why do I need to say something important?
De ce trebuie să spun (eu) ceva important?
I am there with him.
Eu sunt acolo cu el.
I am busy, but I need to be ready soon.
(Eu) Sunt ocupat/ocupată, dar trebuie să fiu gata în curând. [m/f]
I like to work.
(Mie) Îmi place să muncesc.
Who is there?
Cine este acolo?
I want to know if they are here.
(Eu) Vreau să știu dacă ei/ele sunt aici. [masc/fem]
I can go outside.
Eu pot merge afară.
There are seven dolls.
Sunt șapte păpuși.
I do what I want.
(Eu) Fac ce vreau.
Where is the hospital?
Unde este spitalul?

To bring - A aduce
To eat - A mânca
To Drive - A conduce
With me - Cu mine
Without me - Fără mine
How much - Cât
Lunch - Prânz
Fast - Rapid
Quickly - Repede
Slow / slowly - Încet
Inside – În interior
Inside – Înăuntru
Cold - Rece
Hot - Fierbinte
Were – Au fost
When - Când
Only - Numai
Instead - În schimb
Or - Sau
Too (as in too much/excessive) **-** Prea
Many - (m) Mulţi / (f) multe
Much - (m) Mult / (f) multă
A lot - Mulți / multe / mult / multă

How much money do I need to bring with me?
Câţi bani trebuie să aduc cu mine?
Instead of rice, I like bread.
În loc de orez, îmi place pâinea.
Only when you can.
Doar când poţi.
Go there without me.
Du-te acolo fără mine.
I need to drive the car very fast or very slowly.
(Eu) Trebuie să conduc maşina foarte repede sau foarte încet.
It is cold inside of the library.
Este frig în interiorul bibliotecii.
I like to eat a hot meal for my lunch.
(Mie) Îmi place să mănânc o masă caldă la prânz.
The rice has too much salt.
Orezul are prea multă sare.

To answer - A răspunde
To fly - A zbura
To travel - A călători
To learn - A învăța
To swim - A înota
To practice - A practica
To practice - A exersa
To play - a juca
To leave - A pleca
I go to - Mă duc la
First - Primul
Time / Times - Ora/ orele
Like (*preposition*) - Ca
How - Cum
That (conjunction) **–** Că

I need to answer many questions.
(Eu) Trebuie să răspund la multe întrebări.
I want to fly today.
(Eu) Vreau să zbor astăzi.
I need to learn how to swim in the pool.
(Eu) Trebuie să învăț cum să înot în piscină.
I want to learn how to play better tennis.
(Eu) Vreau să învăț cum să joc mai bine tenis.
Everything is about the money.
Totul este despre bani.
I want to leave my dog at home.
(Eu) Vreau să-mi las câinele acasă.
I want to travel the world.
(Eu) Vreau să călătoresc prin lume.
Since the first time.
De prima dată.
The children are yours.
Copiii sunt ai tăi.
I need to know that that is a good idea.
(Eu) Trebuie să știu că aceasta este o idee bună.

*With the knowledge you've gained so far, now try to create your own sentences!

To visit - A vizita
To meet - A (se) întâlni
To give - A da
To walk - A merge
Someone - Cineva
Us - Noi
Mom / Mother – Mama
Nothing - Nimic
Someone - Cineva
No one / nobody - Nimeni
Anyone - Oricine
Against - Împotriva
Which - Care
Just - Doar
Around - În jur
Towards - Spre
Than – Decât
A ride - O cursă

Something is better than nothing.
Ceva este mai bun decât nimic.
I am against him.
Eu sunt împotriva lui.
We go to visit my family each week.
Mergem să vizităm familia mea în fiecare săptămână.
I need to give you something
(Eu) Trebuie să îţi/vă dau ceva. [sing/plu]
Do you want to meet someone?
(Tu) Vrei să întâlneşti pe cineva?
I am here on Wednesdays as well.
Eu sunt aici și miercuri.
You do this everyday?
(Tu) Faci asta zilnic?
You need to walk around the house.
(Tu) Trebuie să te plimbi prin casă. /în jurul casei.
Nobody is here.
Nu este aici.
You can ask anyone for a ride home.
Poți să ceri oricui o cursă până acasă.

To show - A arăta
To prepare - A pregăti
To borrow - A împrumuta
To look like - A arăta ca
To want - A vrea
To stay - A rămâne
To stay - A sta
To continue - A continua
I have – Eu am
I have to - Eu trebuie să
I must - Eu trebuie
I am not going – (Eu) Nu mă duc
Don't / Doesn't - Nu
Friend - Prieten
Grandfather - Bunic
Way (method) **-** Cale
Way (method) **-** Fel
Way (road) - Drum
That's why - De aceea
Incorrect - Incorect
Wrong - Greșit

Do you want to look like Arnold?
Vrei să arăți ca Arnold?
I want to borrow this book for my grandfather.
(Eu) Vreau să împrumut această carte pentru bunicul meu.
I want to drive and to continue on this way to my house.
(Eu) Vreau să conduc și să continui pe acest drum spre casa mea.
I want to stay in Sibiu because I have a friend there.
(Eu) Vreau să stau în Sibiu pentru că am un prieten acolo.
I am not going to see anyone here.
(Eu) Nu am să văd pe nimeni aici.
I need to show you how to prepare breakfast.
(Eu) Trebuie să îți/vă arăt cum să pregatești/pregătiți micul dejun. [sing/plu]
Why don't you have the book?
De ce nu ai cartea?
That is incorrect, I don't need the car today.
Acest lucru este incorect, (eu) nu am nevoie de mașină astăzi.

To remember - A reţine
To remember - A memora
To think - A gândi
To do - A face
To come - A veni
To hear - A auzi
To listen - A asculta
Your – Ta
Grandmother - Bunică
Dark / darkness - Întuneric
Number - Număr
Five - Cinci
Hour - Ora
Minute - Minut
Minutes - Minute
A second - O secunda
A moment - Un moment
Last – Ultima/Ultimul [fem/masc]
More - Mai mult
About - Despre
Music - Muzică

You need to remember your phone number.
Trebuie să îţi aminteşti numărul de telefon.
This is the last hour of darkness.
Aceasta este ultima oră de întuneric.
I want to come with you.
(Eu)Vreau să vin cu tine.
I can hear my grandmother speaking Romanian.
Eu o pot auzi pe bunica mea vorbind română.
I like to listen to music.
Îmi place să ascult muzică.
I need to think about this more.
(Eu)Trebuie să mă gândesc mai mult la asta.
From here until there, it's just five minutes.
De aici până acolo, sunt doar cinci minute.
This is an important moment, even for a second.
Acesta este un moment important, chiar și pentru o secundă.

To leave - A pleca
To turn off - A opri/A închide
To ask - A întreba
To sleep - A dormi
To stop - A opri
To take - A lua
To try - A încerca
To rent - A închiria
Without her - Fără ea
We are - Suntem
English - Engleză
Romanian - Română
Romania - România
United States - Statele Unite
Airport - Aeroport
Permission - Permisiune
Again - Din nou
Same - La fel

He must go and rent a house at the beach.
El trebuie să meargă să închirieze o casă la plajă.
I want to take the test without her.
(Eu)Vreau să fac testul fără ea.
We are here for a long time.
(Noi) Suntem aici de multă vreme.
I need to turn off the lights early tonight.
(Eu) Trebuie să sting luminile devreme diseară/în seara asta.
We want to stop here.
(Noi) Vrem să ne oprim aici.
We are from America.
(Noi) Suntem din America.
Your doctor is in the same building.
Medicul tău/vostru se află/este în aceeaşi clădire. [sg/pl]
In order to leave you have to ask permission.
Pentru a pleca, (tu) trebuie să ceri permisiunea.
I want to go to sleep.
(Eu) Vreau sa ma duc la culcare/Vreau sa mă duc să dorm.
Where is the airport?
Unde este aeroportul?

To open - A deschide
To buy - A cumpăra
To pay - A plăti
To clean - A curăţa
To hope - A spera
To live - A trăi
To return (from place) **-** A reveni/A se întoarce
To return (an object**) -** A returna
Our - Al nostru
Without - Fără
Sister - Soră
Door - Uşă
Nice to meet you - Încântat de cunoştinţă
Name - Nume
Last name –Nume/Nume de familie
Enough - Destul
On the – Pe

I need to open the door for my sister.
(Eu) Trebuie să deschid uşa pentru sora mea.
I need to buy something.
(Eu) Am nevoie să cumpăr ceva.
I want to meet your brothers.
(Eu) Vreau să-i cunosc/întâlnesc pe fraţii tăi.
Nice to meet you, what is your first name and your last name?
Încântat de cunoştinţă, care este prenumele şi numele tău?
We can hope for a better future.
(Noi) Putem spera la un viitor mai bun.
To live without problems is impossible.
A trăi fără probleme este imposibil.
I want to return to Romania.
(Eu) Vreau să mă întorc în România.
Why are you sad right now?
De ce eşti trist acum?
Our house is on the mountain.
Casa noastră este pe munte.

*This *isn't* a phrase book! The purpose of this book is *solely* to provide you with the tools to create *your own* sentences!

To happen - A se întâmpla
To order - A comanda
To drink - A bea
To begin / To start – A începe
To finish - A termina
To help - A ajuta
To smoke - A fuma
To love - A iubi
To talk / to speak - A vorbi
Child - (M) Copil / **(F)** Copilă
Woman - Femeie
Excuse me - Scuzați-mă
Romanian - Română

This needs to happen today.
Asta trebuie să se întâmple astăzi.
Excuse me, my child is here as well.
Scuzați-mă, și copilul meu este aici.
I want to order a soup.
(Eu) Vreau să comand o supă.
We want to start the class soon.
(Noi) Vrem să începem ora (lecția) în curând.
In order to finish at three o'clock this afternoon, I need to finish soon.
Pentru a termina la ora trei în după-amiaza asta, (eu) trebuie să termin în curând.
I want to learn how to speak perfect Romanian.
(Eu) Vreau să învăț să vorbesc perfect limba română.
I don't want to smoke again.
(Eu) Nu vreau să mai fumez din nou.
I want to help.
(Eu) Vreau să ajut.
I love you.
(Eu) Te iubesc.
I see you.
(Eu) Te văd.
I need you.
(Eu) Am nevoie de tine.

To close - A închide
To turn on - A porni
To teach - A învăţa
To teach - A preda
To teach - A instrui
To read - A citi
To write - A scrie
To prefer - A prefera
To choose - A alege
To put - A pune
I talk / I speak - Eu vorbesc
Sun - Soare
Month - Luna
Exact – Exact
Exact – Precis
Less - Mai puţin
Hungarian -

I need this book to learn how to read and write in Romanian.
(Eu) Am nevoie de această carte pentru a învăţa cum să citesc și să scriu în limba română.
I want to teach English in Romania
(Eu) Vreau să predau engleza în România.
I want to turn on the lights and close the door.
(Eu) Vreau să aprind luminile şi să închid uşa.
I want to pay less than you.
(Eu) Vreau să plătesc mai puţin decât tine/voi. [sing/plu]
I prefer to put this here.
(Eu) Prefer să pun asta aici.
I speak with the boy and the girl in Hungarian.
Vorbesc cu băiatul și fata în maghiară.
There is sun outside today.
Astăzi este soare afară.
Is it possible to know the exact date?
Este posibil să știu data exactă?

*With the knowledge you've gained so far, now try to create your own sentences!

To exchange - A schimba
To call - A suna
To sit - A sta
To change - A schimba
To follow - a urma
Him /Her - El/ Ea
Brother - Frate
Dad - Tată
Sky - Cer
Big - Mare
Years - Ani
Up - Sus
Down / below - Jos
Under - Sub
Of course - Desigur
Sorry - Scuze
Welcome - Bine ați/ai venit
During - În timpul
New - Nou
Never - Niciodată
Together - Împreună

I am never able to to exchange this money at the bank.
(Eu) Nu sunt niciodată în stare să schimb acești bani la bancă.
I want to call my brother and my dad today.
(Eu) Vreau să-i sun pe fratele meu și pe tata astăzi.
Of course I can come to the theater, and I want to sit together with you and with your family.
Sigur că pot veni la teatru și vreau să stau împreună cu tine și cu familia ta.
If you look under the table, you can see the new rug.
Dacă te/vă uiți/uitați sub masă, poți/puteți vedea noul covor. [sing/plu]
I can see the sky from the window.
Eu pot vedea cerul de la fereastră.
I am sorry.
Imi pare rau.
The dog wants to follow me to the store.
Câinele vrea să mă urmeze până la magazin.
He is a different man now.
Acum este un om diferit.

To allow - A permite
To believe - A crede
To promise - A promite
To recognize - A recunoaşte
To move - A muta
To enter - A intra
To receive - A primi
Morning - Dimineaţa
Good night - Noapte bună
Good afternoon - Bună ziua
People - Oameni
Man - Bărbat
Free - Gratuit
Far - Departe
Different - Diferit
Throughout - de-a lungul/peste tot
Through - Prin
Except - Cu excepţia

I need to allow him to go with us.
(Eu) Trebuie să-i permit (lui) să meargă cu noi.
I believe everything except this.
Eu cred totul, cu excepţia acestui lucru/mai puţin asta.
Come here quickly.
Vino aici repede.
I must promise to say good night to my parents each night.
(Eu) Trebuie să promit că le spun părinţilor mei noapte bună în fiecare seară.
I can't recognize him.
Eu nu-l pot recunoaşte.
I need to move your cat to a different chair.
Trebuie să îţi/vă mut pisica pe alt scaun. [sing/plu]
They want to enter the competition and receive a free book.
(Ei/Ele) Vor să intre în concurs şi să primească o carte gratuită. [fem/masc]
I see the sun throughout the morning from the kitchen.
Eu văd soarele toată dimineaţa din bucătărie.
I go into the house from the front entrance and not through the yard.
(Eu) Intru în casă pe intrarea din faţă şi nu prin curte.

To wish - A dori
To get - A lua
To forget - A uita
To feel - A simți
To like - A place
Everybody – Toți/Toată lumea
Person - Persoană
Restaurant - Restaurant
Bathroom - Baie
Goodbye - La revedere / **See you soon -** Ne vedem curând
Next (following) – Următorul
Next (near close) – Lânga
In front - În față / **Behind –** În spate
Bad - Rău
Although - Deși
Great – Grozav/Mare
Well - Bine

I don't want to wish you anything bad.
(Eu) Nu vreau să îți/vă doresc nimic rău.
I must forget everybody from my past.
(Eu) Trebuie să uit pe toată lumea din trecutul meu.
I am next to the person behind you.
Eu sunt lângă persoana din spatele tău.
To feel well I must take vitamins.
Pentru a mă simți bine (eu) trebuie să iau vitamine.
There is a great person in front of me.
În fața mea este o persoană grozavă.
Goodbye my friend.
La revedere, prietenul meu.
Which is the best restaurant in the area?
Care este cel mai bun restaurant din zonă?
I can feel the heat.
Eu pot simți căldura.
I need to repair a part of the cabinet bathroom.
(Eu) Am nevoie să repar o parte din dulapul din baie.
She must get a car before the next year.
(Ea) Trebuie să ia o mașină până la anul.
I want to like the house, but it is very small.
(Eu) Vreau să-mi placă casa, dar este foarte mică.

To remove - A elimina/A scoate
To check - A verifica
To hold - A ţine
Belong - Aparţine
Week - Săptămâna
Beautiful - Frumos
Please - Vă rog
Price - Preţ
To include - A include
Including - Inclusiv
Small - Mic
Real – Adevărat/Real
Size - Dimensiune
Even though - Chiar dacă
So (as in *then*) **-** Deci
So (so as in *so much*) **-** Atât

She wants to remove this door please.
Ea vrea să scoata această uşă, te rog.
This doesn't belong here, I need to check again.
Aceasta nu este de aici, (eu) trebuie să verific din nou.
This week the weather was very beautiful.
Săptămâna aceasta vremea a fost foarte frumoasă.
Is that a real diamond?
Este acesta un diamant adevărat?
We need to check the size of the house.
Trebuie să verificăm dimensiunea casei.
Can you please put the wood in the fire?
Poţi/puteţi, te rog/vă rog, să pui/puneţi lemnul pe/în foc? [sing/plu]
Can you please hold my hand?
Poţi, te rog, sa ma ţii de mână?
The sun is high in the sky.
Soarele este sus pe cer.
I can pay this although the price is expensive.
Eu pot plăti acest lucru deşi preţul este scump.
Including everything is this price correct?
Incluzând totul, este corect acest preţ?

*In Romanian, the adjective beautiful / frumos has four different tenses. Masculine: frumos / (plural) frumoşi. Feminine: frumoasă / (plural) frumoase.

Building Bridges

In Building Bridges, we take six conjugated verbs that have been selected after studies I have conducted for several months in order to determine which verbs are most commonly conjugated, and which are then automatically followed by an infinitive verb. For example, once you know how to say, "I need," "I want," "I can," and "I like," you will be able to connect words and say almost anything you want more correctly and understandably. The following three pages contain these six conjugated verbs in first, second, third, fourth, and fifth person, as well as some sample sentences. Please master the entire program up until *here* prior to venturing onto this section.

I want - Eu vreau
I need – (Eu) Am nevoie
I can - Eu pot
I like - Îmi place
I go - Eu plec
I have - Eu am
I have to - Eu trebuie să
I must – Eu trebuie

I want to go to my house.
(Eu) Vreau să merg la casa mea.

I can go with you to the bus station.
(Eu) Pot să merg cu tine la stația de autobuz.

I need to walk outside the museum.
(Eu) Am nevoie/Trebuie să merg în afara muzeului.

I like to eat oranges.
(Mie) Îmi place să mănânc portocale.

I am going to teach a class.
(Eu) O să predau un curs.

I have to speak to my teacher.
(Eu) Trebuie să vorbesc cu profesorul meu.

Please master *every* single page up until here prior to attempting the following pages!

You want / do you want - Tu vrei / vrei tu?
He wants / does he want - El vrea / vrea el?
She wants / does she want - Ea vrea / vrea ea?
We want / do we want - Noi vrem / vrem noi?
They want / do they want – Ei/ele vor / vor ei/ele?
You (plural) want - Voi vreţi/ vreţi voi?

You need / do you need - Tu ai nevoie /ai nevoie tu?
He needs / does he need - El are nevoie / are nevoie el?
She needs / does she need - Ea are nevoie / are nevoie ea?
We want / do we want - Noi vrem / vrem noi?
They need / do they need – Ei/ele au nevoie / au nevoie ei/ele?

You (plural) need - Voi aveţi nevoie/ aveţi nevoie voi
You can / can you - Tu poţi / poţi tu?
He can / can he - El poate / poate el?
She can / can she - Ea poate / poate ea?
We can / can we - Noi putem / putem noi?
They can / can they – Ei/ele pot / pot ei/ele?
You (plural) can - Voi puteţi
You like / do you like - ţie îţi place / îţi place ţie?
He likes / does he like – Lui îi place / îi place lui?
She likes / does she like – Ei îi place / îi place ei?
We like / do we like – Nouă ne place / ne place nouă?
They like / do they like – Lor le place / le place lor?
You (plural) like - Vouă vă place

You go / do you go – Tu mergi / mergi tu?
He goes / does he go – El merge / merge el?
She goes / does she go – Ea merge / merge ea?
We go / do we go – Noi mergem / mergem noi?
They go / do they go – Ei/Ele merg / merg ei/ele?
You (plural) go - Voi mergeţi

You have / do you have - Tu ai / ai tu?
He has / does he have – El are / are el?
She has / does she have – Ea are / are ea?
We have / do we have – Noi avem / avem noi?
They have / do they have – Ei/ele au / au ei/ele?

Do you want to go?
(Tu) Vrei sa mergi?/(Voi) Vreţi să mergeţi? [sing/plu]

Does he want to fly?
Vrea el să zboare?

We want to swim.
(Noi) Vrem să înotăm.

Do they want to run?
Vor ei/ele să alerge?

Do you need to clean?
(Tu) Trebuie să cureţi?

She needs to sing a song.
Ea trebuie să cânte un cântec.

We need to travel.
(Noi) Avem nevoie să călătorim.

They don't need to fight
Nu e nevoie ca ei să se lupte/certe. [not synonyms]

You (plural) need to save your money.
Voi trebuie sa vă economisiti banii.

Can you hear me?
(Tu) Mă poţi auzi?

He can dance very well.
El poate dansa foarte bine.

We can go out tonight.
(Noi) Putem ieşi diseară.

The fireman can break the door during an emergency.
Pompierul poate sparge uşa în timpul unei urgenţe.

Do you like to eat here?
(ţie) Îţi place să mănânci aici?

He likes to spend time here.
Lui îi place să petreacă timpul aici.

We like to stay in the house.
(Nouă) Ne place să stăm în casă.

They like to cook.
(Lor) Le place să gătească.

You (plural) like to play soccer.
Vouă vă place să julcati fotbal.

Do you go to the movies on weekends?
(Tu) Mergi la filme în weekend-uri?

He goes fishing.
El merge la pescuit.

We are going to relax.
Noi o să ne relaxam.

They go out to eat at a restaurant every day.
Ei/ele ies zilnic să mănânce la un restaurant. [sing/plu]

Do you have money?
(Tu) Ai bani?

She has to look outside.
Ea trebuie să privească afară.

We have to sign our names.
(Noi) Trebuie să ne semnăm.

They have to send the letter.
Ei/Ele trebuie să trimită scrisoarea.

You (plural) have to stand in line.
Voi trebuie să stati în linie.

Other Useful Tools in the Romanian Language

Days of the Week - Zilele săptămânii
Sunday - Duminică
Monday - Luni
Tuesday - Marţi
Wednesday - Miercuri
Thursday - Joi
Friday - Vineri
Saturday - Sambata

Seasons - Anotimpuri
Spring - Primăvara / **Summer -** Vara
Autumn - Toamna / **Winter -** Iarna

Colors – Culori
Black - Negru
White - Alb
Gray - Gri
Red - Roşu
Blue - Albastru
Yellow - Galben
Green - Verde
Orange - Portocaliu
Purple – Violet/Purpuriu
Brown - Maro

Numbers - Numere
One - Unu
Two – Doi
Three - Trei
Four - Patru
Five - Cinci
Six - şase
Seven - şapte
Eight - Opt
Nine - Nouă
Ten - Zece

Cardinal Directions - Direcţii cardinale
North - Nord **/ South -** Sud
East - Est / **West -** Vest

Conclusion

Congratulations! You have completed all the tools needed to master the Romanian language, and I hope that this has been a valuable learning experience. Now you have sufficient communication skills to be confident enough to embark on a visit to Sweden, impress your friends, and boost your resume so *good luck*.

This program is available in other languages as well, and it is my fervent hope that my language learning programs will be used for good, enabling people from all corners of the globe and from all cultures and religions to be able to communicate harmoniously. After memorizing the required three hundred and fifty words, please perform a daily five-minute exercise by creating sentences in your head using these words. This simple exercise will help you grasp conversational communications even more effectively. Also, once you memorize the vocabulary on each page, follow it by using a notecard to cover the words you have just memorized and test yourself and follow *that* by going back and using this same notecard technique on the pages you studied during the previous days. This repetition technique will assist you in mastering these words in order to provide you with the tools to create your own sentences.

Every day, use this notecard technique on the words that you have just studied.

Everything in life has a catch. The catch here is just consistency. If you just open the book, and after the first few pages of studying the program, you put it down, then you will not gain anything. However, if you consistently dedicate a half hour daily to studying, as well as reviewing what you have learned from previous days, then you will quickly realize why this method is the most effective technique ever created to become conversational in a foreign language. My technique works! For anyone who doubts this technique, all I can say is that it has worked for me and hundreds of others.

Conversational Romanian Quick and Easy

The Most Innovative Technique to Learn the Romanian Language

Part II

YATIR NITZANY

Introduction to the Program

In the first book, you were taught the 350 most useful words in the Romanian language, which, once memorized, could be combined in order for you to create your own sentences. Now, with the knowledge you have gained, you can use those words in Conversational Romanian Quick and Easy Part 2 and Part 3, in order to supplement the 350 words that you've already memorized. This combination of words and sentences will help you master the language to even greater proficiency and quicker than with other courses.

The books that comprise Parts 2 and 3 have progressed from just vocabulary and are now split into various categories that are useful in our everyday lives. These categories range from travel to food to school and work, and other similarly broad subjects. In contrast to various other methods, the topics that are covered also contain parts of vocabulary that are not often broached, such as the military, politics, and religion. With these more unusual topics for learning conversational languages, the student can learn quicker and easier. This method is flawless and it has proven itself time and time again.

If you decide to travel to Romania, then this book will help you speak the Romanian language.

This method has worked for me and thousands of others. It surpasses any other language-learning method system currently on the market today.

This book, Part 2, specifically deals with practical aspects concerning travel, camping, transportation, city living, entertainment such as films, food including vegetables and fruit, shopping, family including grandparents, in-laws, and stepchildren, human anatomy, health, emergencies, and natural disasters, and home situations.

The sentences within each category can help you get by in other countries.

In relation to travel, for example, you are given sentences about food, airport necessities such as immigration, and passports. Helpful phrases include, "Where is the immigration and passport control inside the airport?" and "I want to order a bowl of cereal and toast with jelly." For flights there are informative combinations such as, "There is a long line of passengers in the terminal because of the delay on the runway." When arriving in another country options for what to say include, "We want to hire a driver for the tour. However, we want to pay with a credit card instead of cash" and, "On which street is the car-rental agency?

When discussing entertainment in another country and in a new language, you are provided with sentences and vocabulary that will help you interact with others. You can discuss art galleries and watching foreign films. For example, you may need to say to friends, "I need subtitles if I watch a foreign film" and, 'The mystery-suspense genre films are usually good movies'. You can talk about your own filming experience in front of the camera.

The selection of topics in this book is much wider than in ordinary courses. By including social issue such as incarceration, it will help you to engage with more people who speak the language you are learning.

Part 3 will deal with vocabulary and sentences relevant to indoor matters such as school and the office, but also a variety of professions and sports.

TRAVEL - VOIAJ

Flight - Zbor
Airplane - Avion
Airport – Aeroport
Terminal - Terminal
Passport - Paşaport/ **Customs** - Vama
Take off (airplane) – Decolare (avion)/ **Landing** - Aterizare
Departure - Plecare/ **Arrival** – Sosire
Gate - Poarta
Luggage - Bagaje/ **Suitcase** - Valiză
Baggage claim - Recuperarea bagajelor
Passenger – Pasager
Final Destination – Destinație Finală
Boarding - Îmbarcare
Runway - Pistă
Line - Linie
Delay - Întârziere
Wing - Aripă

I enjoy traveling.
Îmi place să călătoresc.
This is a very expensive flight.
Acesta este un zbor foarte costisitor.
The airplane takes off in the morning and lands at night.
Avionul decolează dimineața și aterizează noaptea.
My suitcase is at the baggage claim.
Valiza mea se află la preluarea bagajelor..
We need to go to the departure gate instead of the arrival gate.
Trebuie să mergem la poarta de plecare în loc de poarta de sosire.
There is a long line of passengers in the terminal because of the delay on the runway.
Este o coadă lungă de pasageri în terminal din cauza întârzierii pe pistă.
What is your final destination?
Care este destinația ta finală?
I don't like to sit above the wing of the airplane.
Nu-mi place să stau deasupra aripii avionului.
The flight takes off at 3pm, but the boarding commences at 2:20pm.
Zborul decolează la ora 15:00, dar îmbarcarea începe la ora 14:20.
Where is the passport control inside the airport?
Unde se face controlul pașapoartelor în interiorul aeroportului?
I am almost finished at customs.
Aproape am terminat la vamă.

International flight – Zbor internațional/ **Domestic flight –** Zbor intern
Business class – Clasa business
First class – Clasa I
Economy class – Clasa economică
Round trip - Dus-întors / **Direct flight -** Zbor direct
One-way flight - Zbor dus
Return flight - Zbor de întoarcere
Flight attendant - Însoțitor de zbor
Layover / connection - Escală/ legătură
Reservation - Rezervare
Security check – Verificare de securitate
Checked bags - Bagaje de cală/ **Carry on bag –** Bagaj de mână
Business trip - Călătorie de afaceri
Check in counter – Ghișeu de check-in
Travel agency - Agentie de turism
Visa - Viză / **Country –** Țară
Temporary visa – Viză temporară /**Permanent visa –** Viză permanentă

The flight attendant told me to go to the check in counter.
Însoțitorul de bord mi-a spus să mă duc la ghișeul de check-in.
For international flights, you must be at the airport at least three hours before the flight.
Pentru zborurile internaționale, trebuie să fiți la aeroport cu cel puțin trei ore înainte de zbor.
For a domestic flight, I need to arrive at the airport at least two hours before the flight.
Pentru un zbor intern, trebuie să ajung la aeroport cu cel puțin două ore înainte de zbor.
Business class is usually cheaper than first class.
Clasa business este de obicei mai ieftină decât clasa întâi.
A one-way ticket is cheaper than the round-trip ticket at the travel agency.
Un bilet dus este mai ieftin decât biletul dus-întors la agenția de turism.
I prefer a direct flight without a layover.
Prefer un zbor direct fără escală.
I must reserve my return flight.
Trebuie să-mi rezerv zborul de întoarcere.
Why do I need to remove my shoes at the security check?
De ce trebuie să-mi scot pantofii la controlul de securitate?
I have three checked bags and one carry-on.
Am trei bagaje de cală și un bagaj de mână.
I have to ask my travel agent if this country requires a visa.
Trebuie să-mi întreb agentul de turism dacă această țară necesită viză.

Trip – Excursie
Tourist - Turist/ **Tourism -** Turism
Holiday - Vacanţă
Vacations - Vacanţe
Currency exchange - Schimb valutar
Port of entry - Port de intrare
Car rental agency - Agentie de inchirieri auto
Identification - Identificare
GPS - GPS
Road - Drum / **Map -** Hartă
Information center - Centru de informare
Bank - Bancă
Hotel – Hotel / **Motel -** Motel / **Hostel -** Hostel
Leisure - Agrement
Driver – Șofer
Credit - Credit / **Cash -**Numerar
A guide - Un ghid / **Tour -** Tur
Ski resort - Stațiune de schi

I had an amazing trip.
Am avut o călătorie uimitoare.
The currency exchange counter is past the port of entry.
Ghişeul de schimb valutar este după portul de intrare.
There is a lot of tourism during the holidays and vacations.
Este mult turism în perioada sărbătorilor și vacanțelor.
Where is the car-rental agency?
Unde este agenţia de închirieri auto?
You need to show your identification.
Trebuie să-ţi arăţi actul de identitate.
It's more convenient to use the GPS on the roads instead of a map.
Este mai convenabil să folosiţi GPS-ul pe drumuri în loc de o hartă.
Why is the information center closed today?
De ce este centrul de informare închis astăzi?
When I am in a foreign country, I go to the bank before I go to the hotel.
Când sunt într-o ţară străină, merg la bancă înainte de a merge la hotel.
I need to book my leisure vacation at the ski resort today.
Trebuie să-mi rezerv astăzi concediul de odihnă în stațiunea de schi.
We want to hire a driver for the tour.
Vrem să angajăm un şofer pentru tur.
We want to pay with a credit card instead of cash.
Dorim să plătim cu un card de credit în loc de numerar.
Does the tour include an English-speaking guide?
Turul include un ghid vorbitor de limba engleză?

TRANSPORTATION - TRANSPORT

Car - Maşină
Bus - Autobuz
Train - Tren/ **Train station -** Gară
Train tracks - Şine de tren/ **Train cart -** Cărucior de tren
Taxi - Taxi
Subway - Metrou
Motorcycle - Motocicletă/ **Scooter -** Trotinetă
Station - Gară
Helicopter - Elicopter
School bus – Autobuz şcolar
Limousine - Limuzină
Driver license - Permis de conducere
Vehicle registration - Înmatricularea vehiculelor
License plate - Plăcuță de înmatriculare
Ticket - Bilet **/ Ticket** (penalty) – Amendă (sancțiune)

Where is the public transportation?
Unde este transportul public?
Where can I buy a bus ticket?
De unde pot cumpăra un bilet de autobuz?
Please call a taxi.
Vă rugăm să chemați un taxi.
In some cities, you don't need a car because you can rely on the subway.
În unele orașe, nu aveți nevoie de o mașină pentru că vă puteți baza pe metrou.
Where is the train station?
Unde este gara?
The train cart is still stuck on the tracks.
Vagonul de tren este încă blocat pe șine..
The motorcycles make loud noises.
Motocicletele scot zgomote puternice.
Where can I rent a scooter?
Unde pot închiria un scuter?
I want to plan a helicopter tour.
Vreau să planific un tur cu elicopterul.
I want to go to the party in a limousine.
Vreau să merg la petrecere într-o limuzină.
Don't forget to bring your driver's license and registration.
Nu uitați să vă aduceți permisul de conducere și certificatul de înmatriculare..
The cop gave me a ticket because my license plate has expired.
Polițistul mi-a dat o amendă pentru că mi-a expirat plăcuța de înmatriculare.

Truck – Camion/ **Pickup truck -** Camionă
Bicycle – Bicicletă
Van - Microbuz
Gas station – Benzinărie
Gasoline - Benzină
Tire - Pneu
Oil change – Schimbarea uleiului
Tire change – Schimbarea anvelopelor
Mechanic – Mecanic
Canoe - Canoe
Ship - Navă/ **Boat –** Barcă
Yacht - Iaht
Sailboat - Barcă cu pânze
Motorboat - Barcă cu motor
Marina – Port / **The dock -** Portul
Cruise - Croazieră/ **Cruise ship -** Nava de croazieră
Ferry - Feribot
Submarine - Submarin

I can put my bicycle in my truck.
Îmi pot pune bicicleta în camion.
Where is the gas station?
Unde este benzinăria?
I need gasoline and also to put air in my tires.
Am nevoie de benzină şi, de asemenea, să îmi umflu cauciucurile.
I need to take my car to the mechanic for a tire and oil change.
Trebuie să-mi duc maşina la mecanic pentru un schimb de anvelope şi ulei.
I can put my canoe in the van.
Îmi pot pune canoea în dubă.
Can I bring my yacht to the boat show at the marina?
Pot să-mi aduc iahtul la expoziţia de ambarcaţiuni de la port?
I prefer a motorboat instead of a sailboat.
Prefer o barcă cu motor în locule unei bărci cu pânze.
I want to leave my boat at the dock on the island.
Vreau să-mi las barca la portul de pe insulă.
This spot is a popular stopping point for the cruise ship.
Acest loc este un punct de oprire popular pentru vasul de croazieră.
This was an excellent cruise.
Aceasta a fost o croazieră excelentă.
Do you have the schedule for the ferry?
Ai programul feribotului?
The submarine is yellow.
Submarinul este galben.

CITY - ORAȘ

Town - Oraș/ **Village** - Sat
House / home – Casă
Apartment - Apartament
Building - Clădire / **Skyscraper –** Zgârie-nori
Highrise building - Clădire înaltă /**Tower** - Turn
Neighborhood – Cartier
Office building – Clădire de birouri
Post office – Oficiu postal
Location - Locație
Elevator – Lift/ **Stairs** - Scări
Fence - Gard
Construction site – Șantier
Bridge - Pod
Gate - Poartă
City hall – Primarie/ **Mayor** - Primar
Fire department – Departamentul de pompieri

Is this a city or a village?
Acesta este un oraș sau un sat?
Does he live in a house or an apartment?
Locuiește într-o casă sau într-un apartament?
This residential building does not have an elevator, just stairs.
Această clădire rezidențială nu are lift, doar scări.
These skyscrapers are located in the center city.
Acești zgârie-nori sunt situati în centrul orașului.
The tower is tall but the building beside it is very short.
Turnul este înalt, dar clădirea de lângă el este foarte scurtă.
This is a beautiful neighborhood.
Acesta este un cartier frumos.
There is a fence around the construction site.
Există un gard în jurul șantierului.
The post office is located in that office building.
Oficiul poștal este situat în acea clădire de birouri.
The bridge is closed today.
Podul este închis astăzi.
The gate is open.
Poarta este deschisă.
The fire department is located in the building next to city hall.
Secția de pompieri se află în clădirea de lângă primărie.
The mayor of Cluj-Napoca is very well known.
Primarul din Cluj-Napoca este foarte cunoscut.

Street - Stradă/ **Main street -** Stradă principală / **Sidewalk -** Trotuar
To park - A parca / **Parking lot -** Parcare
Traffic - Trafic / **Traffic light -** Semafor
Red light – Lumină roşie/ **Yellow light –** Lumină galbenă
Green light – Lulmină verde
Lane - Lane / **Toll lane -** Drum cu taxă
Fast lane – Bandă rapidă / **Slow lane –** Bandă lentă
Right lane – Banda din dreapta/ **Left lane –** Banda din stânga
Highway – Autostradă/ **Intersection -** Intersecție/ **Tunnel –** Tunel
U-turn - Întoarcere/ **Shortcut -** Comandă rapidă / **Bypass -** Ocolire
Stop sign - Indicator de oprire
Pedestrians - Pietoni/ **Crosswalk -** Trecere de pietoni

The parking is on the main street and not on the sidewalk.
Parcarea este pe strada principală şi nu pe trotuar.
Where is the parking lot?
Unde este parcarea?
The traffic is very bad today.
Traficul este foarte prost azi.
You must avoid the fast lane because it's a toll lane.
Trebuie să evitați banda rapidă deoarece este o bandă cu taxă.
We don't like to drive on the highway.
Nu ne place să conducem pe autostradă.
At a red light you need to stop, at a yellow light you must be prepared to stop and at a green you can drive.
La un semafor roşu trebuie să te opreşti, la un semafor galben trebuie să fii pregătit să opreşti şi la un semafor verde poți conduce.
This road has too many traffic lights.
Acest drum are prea multe semafoare.
At the intersection, we need to stay in the left lane instead of the right lane because that's a bus lane.
La intersecție, trebuie să rămânem pe banda din stânga în loc de banda din dreapta, deoarece aceasta este o bandă de autobuz.
The tunnel seems longer than yesterday.
Tunelul pare mai lung decât ieri.
It's a short drive.
Este un drum scurt.
The next bus stop is far away from here.
Următoarea stație de autobuz este departe de aici.
You need to turn right at the stop sign and then continue on straight.
Trebuie să virezi la dreapta la semnul de oprire şi apoi să continui drept.
The pedestrians use the crosswalk to cross the road.
Pietonii folosesc trecerea de pietoni pentru a traversa drumul.

Capital – Capitală
Resort - Stațiune
Port - Port
Road - Drum**/ Trail, path –** Alee, potecă
Bus station - Autogară**/ Bus stop –** Stație de autobuz
Night club – Club de noapte
Downtown – Centrul orașului
District - Sector/ **County -** Județ
Statue - Statuie**/ Monument -** Monument
Castle – Castel **/ Church -** Biserică/ **Cathedral -** Catedrală
Synagogue - Sinagogă/ **Mosque -** Moschee
Science museum – Muzeul științei **/ Zoo –** Grădină Zoologică
Playground – Loc de joacă **/ Swimming pool –** Piscina
Jail / Prison - Închisoare

The capital is a major attraction point for tourists.
Capitala este un punct de atracție major pentru turiști.
The resort is next to the port.
Statiunea este langa port.
The night club is located in the downtown area.
Clubul de noapte este situat în centrul orașului.
In which district do you live in?
In ce sector locuiesti?
This statue is a city monument.
Această statuie este un monument al orașului.
This is an ancient castle.
Acesta este un castel antic.
Where is the local church?
Unde este biserica locală?
That is a beautiful cathedral.
Aceea este o catedrală frumoasă.
Do you want to go to the zoo or the science museum?
Vrei să mergi la grădina zoologică sau la muzeul științei?
The children are in the playground.
Copiii sunt în locul de joacă.
The swimming pool is closed for the community today.
Piscina este închisă pentru comunitate astăzi.
You need to follow the trail alongside the main street to reach the bus station.
Trebuie să urmați dri,iș de lângă strada principală pentru a ajunge la stația de autobuz.
There is a jail in this county, but not a prison.
În acest județ există o închisoare, dar nu și un penitenciar.

ENTERTAINMENT - DIVERTISMENT

Film / movie - Film
Theater (movie theater) - Teatru
Actor - Actor/ **Actress** - Actriță
Genre – Gen / **Subtitles** – Subtitrări
Action film - Film de acțiune
Foreign film - Film străin
Mystery film – Film cu mistere
Suspense film – Film de suspans
Documentary film - Film documentar
Biography - Biografie
Drama film - Film dramatic
Comedy film - Film de comedie
Romance film - Film de dragoste
Horror film - Film de groază
Animation film - Film de animație/ **Cartoon** – Desen animat
Director – Regzor / **Producer** - Producător / **Audience** – Public

There are three new movies at the theater that I want to see.
Sunt trei filme noi la teatru pe care vreau să le văd.
He is a really good actor.
Este un actor cu adevărat bun.
She is an excellent actress.
Este o actriță excelentă.
That was a good action movie.
A fost un film de acțiune bun.
We need subtitles if we watch a foreign film.
Avem nevoie de subtitrări dacă ne uităm la un film străin.
Mystery or suspense films are usually good movies.
Filmele cu mister sau suspans sunt de obicei filme bune.
I like documentary films. However, comedy-drama or romance films are better.
Îmi plac filmele documentare. Cu toate acestea, filmele de comedie-dramă sau de dragoste sunt mai bune.
Sometimes biographies are boring to watch.
Uneori, biografiile sunt plictisitoare de urmărit.
I like to watch horror movies.
Îmi place să mă uit la filme de groază.
It's fun to watch animated movies.
Este distractiv să vizionezi filme animate.
The director and the producer can meet the audience today.
Regizorul și producătorul se pot întâlni astăzi cu publicul.

Entertainment - Divertisment
Television - Televiziune
A show (as in television) **-** O emisiune
A show (as in live performance) **-** Un spectacol
Channel – Canal
Series (in television) **-** Serial
Commercial - Reclamă
Episode - Episodul
Anchorman - Prezentator
Anchorwoman - Prezentatoare
News - Știri
News station – Post de știri
Screening - Verificare
Live broadcast - Transmisiune live
Broadcast - Difuzare
Headline - Titlu
Viewer – Spectator
Speech – Discurs
Script - Scenariu
Screen - Ecran
Camera - Cameră

It's time to buy a new television.
Este timpul să cumperi un televizor nou.
This was the first episode of this television show yet it was a long series.
Acesta a fost primul episod al acestei emisiuni de televiziune, dar a fost un serial lung.
There aren't any commercials on this channel.
Nu există reclame pe acest canal.
This anchorman and anchorwoman work for our local news station.
Prezentatorul și prezentatoarea lucrează pentru postul nostru local de știri.
They decided to screen a live broadcast on the news.
Au decis să difuzeze o emisiune în direct la știri.
The news station featured the headlines before the program began.
Postul de știri a prezentat titlurile înainte de începerea programului.
Tonight, all the details about the incident were mentioned on the news.
În această seară, toate detaliile despre incident au fost menționate la știri.
The viewers wanted to hear the presidential speech today.
Telespectatorii au vrut să audă astăzi discursul prezidențial.
I must read my script in front of the screen and the camera
Trebuie să-mi citesc scenariul în fața ecranului și a camerei
We want to enjoy the entertainment this evening.
Vrem să ne bucurăm de divertisment în această seară.

Theater (play) – (Piesă de) **Teatru**
A musical - Un musical
A play - O piesă
Stage – Scenă/ **Audition** - Audiție
Performance – Performanță (Spectacol)
Box office - Box-office/ **Ticket** – Bilet
Singer – (m) Cântăreț, (f) Cântăreață / **Band** – Trupă
Orchestra - Orchestră
Opera - Operă
Music - Muzică
Song - Cântec
Musical instrument – Instrument muzical
Drum - Tobă
Guitar - Chitară
Piano - Pian
Trumpet – Trompetă
Violin – Vioară
Flute - Flaut
Art - Artă
Gallery - Galerie
Studio - Studio
Museum – Muzeu

It was a great musical performance.
A fost un spectacol muzical grozav.
Can I perform for the play on this stage?
Pot cânta pentru piesă pe această scenă?
She is the lead singer of the band.
Ea este solistul trupei.
I will go to the box office tomorrow to purchase tickets for the opera.
Mă duc mâine la casa de bilete să cumpăr bilete pentru operă.
The orchestra needs to perform below the stage.
Orchestra trebuie să cânte sub scenă.
I like to listen to this type of music. I hope to hear a good song.
Îmi place să ascult acest tip de muzică. Sper să aud o melodie bună.
The common musical instruments that are used in a concert are drums, guitars, pianos, trumpets, violins, and flutes.
Instrumentele muzicale uzuale care sunt folosite într-un concert sunt tobe, chitare, piane, trompete, viori și flaut.
The art gallery has a studio for rent.
Galeria de artă are un studio de închiriat.
I went to an art museum yesterday.
Ieri am fost la un muzeu de artă.

FOODS - ALIMENTE / MÂNCARE

Grocery store - Magazin alimentar
Market - Piață**/ Supermarket -** Supermarket
Groceries - Produse alimentare
Butcher shop - Macelarie/ **Butcher -** Măcelar
Bakery - Brutărie/ **Baker -** Brutar
Breakfast – Mic dejun**/ Lunch –** Pranz**/ Dinner –** Cina
Meat - Carne**/ Chicken -** Pui
Seafood – Fructe de mare
Egg – Ou/ (plural) Ouă
Milk - Lapte**/ Butter –** Unt **/ Cheese -** Brânză
Bread - Pâine **/ Flour -** Făină **/ Oil -** Ulei
Baked - La cuptor **/ Cake -** Tort
Beer - Bere**/ Wine –** Vin
Cinnamon - Scorțișoară
Powder - Pulbere
Mustard - Mustar

*In Romanian *mâncare* is the general word for "food", while *alimente* refers to groceries and food products.

Where is the nearest grocery store?
Unde este cel mai apropiat magazin alimentar?
Where can I buy meat and chicken?
De unde pot cumpăra carne și pui?
We need to buy flour, eggs, milk, butter, and oil to bake my cake.
Trebuie să cumpărăm făină, ouă, lapte, unt și ulei pentru a-mi coace tortul.
The groceries are already in the car.
Alimentele sunt deja în mașină.
We drink beer or wine during the meal.
Bem bere sau vin în timpul mesei.
The rolls are covered with cinnamon.
Rulourile sunt acoperite cu scorțișoară.
The butcher shop is near the bakery.
Macelaria este lângă brutarie.
I have to go to the market, to buy a half kilo of meat.
Trebuie să merg la piață, să cumpăr o jumătate de kilogram de carne.
For lunch, we can eat seafood, and pasta for dinner.
La prânz, putem mânca fructe de mare și paste la cină.
I usually eat bread with a slice of cheese for breakfast.
De obicei mănânc pâine cu o felie de brânză la micul dejun.
I like ketchup and mustard on my hotdog.
Îmi plac ketchup-ul și muștarul pe hotdog-ul meu.

Menu - Meniu
Beef - Carne de vită/ **Lamb** - Miel/ **Pork** - Carne de porc
Steak - Friptură
Fish – Peşte
Hamburger - Hamburger
Water – Apă
Salad - Salată
Soup - Supă
Appetizer – Aperitiv/ **Entrée** – Entrée
Cooked - Gătită
Boiled - Fiert/ **Fried** - Prăjit
Grilled - La grătar/ **Broiled** - Gratinat
Raw - Crud
Dessert – Desert
Ice cream - Îngheţată
Coffee – Cafea/ **Tea** – Ceai
Olive oil – Ulei de măsline
Juice - Suc
Honey - Miere / **Sugar** - Zahăr

Do you have a menu in English?
Aveţi un meniu in limba engleza?
Which is preferable, the fried fish or the grilled lamb?
Ce este de preferat, peştele prăjit sau mielul la grătar?
I want to order a cup of water, a soup for my appetizer, and pizza for my entrée.
Vreau să comand o cană de apă, o supă pentru aperitiv şi pizza ca antreu.
I want to order a steak for myself, a hamburger for my son, and ice cream for my wife.
Vreau să comand o friptură pentru mine, un hamburger pentru fiul meu şi îngheţată pentru soţia mea.
What type of dessert is included with my coffee?
Ce tip de desert este inclus cu cafeaua mea?
Can I order a salad with a hard boiled egg and olive oil on the side?
Pot comanda o salată cu un ou fiert tare şi ulei de măsline ca garnitură?
Is the piece of fish in the sushi cooked or raw?
Bucata de peşte din sushi este gătită sau crudă?
I want to order a fruit juice instead of a soda.
Vreau să comand un suc de fructe în loc de un suc.
I want to order tea with a teaspoon of honey instead of sugar.
Vreau să comand ceai cu o linguriţă de miere în loc de zahăr.
The tip is 15% at this restaurant.
Bacşişul este de 15% la acest restaurant.

Vegetarian - Vegetarian
Vegan – Vegan
Dairy - Lactate/ **Dairy products** - Produse lactate
Salt - Sare/ **Pepper** - Piper
Flavor - Aromă
Spices - Condimente
Nuts - Nuci / **Peanuts** - Arahide
Sauce - Sos
Sandwich - Sandviș
Mayonnaise - Maioneză
Rice - Orez
Fries - Cartofi prajiti
Soy - Soia
Jelly - Jeleu
Chocolate - Ciocolată/ **Cookie** - Prăjitură/ **A candy** - O bomboană
Whipped cream - Friscă
Popsicle - Acadea
Frozen - Congelată/ **Thawed** – Dezghețat

I don't eat meat because I am a vegetarian.
Nu mănânc carne pentru că sunt vegetarian.
My brother won't eat dairy products because he is a vegan.
Fratele meu nu va mânca produse lactate pentru că este vegan.
Food tastes much better with salt, pepper, and other spices.
Mâncarea are un gust mult mai bun cu sare, piper și alte condimente.
The only things I have in my freezer are popsicles.
Singurele lucruri pe care le am în congelator sunt acadelele.
No chocolate, candy, or whipped cream until after dinner.
Fără ciocolată, bomboane sau frișcă până după cină.
I want to try a sample of that piece of cheese.
Vreau să încerc o mostră din bucata aceea de brânză.
I have allergies to nuts and peanuts.
Sunt alergic la nuci și alune.
This sauce is delicious.
Acest sos este delicios.
Why do you always put mayonnaise on your sandwich?
De ce-ți pui mereu maioneză pe sandviș?
The food is still frozen so we need to wait for it to thaw.
Mâncarea este încă congelată, așa că trebuie să așteptăm să se dezghețe.
Please bring me a bowl of cereal and a slice of toasted bread with jelly.
Vă rog să-mi aduceți un castron de cereale și o felie de pâine prăjită cu jeleu.
It's healthier to eat rice than fries.
Este mai sănătos să mănânci orez decât cartofi prăjiți.

VEGETABLES - LEGUME

Eggplant - Vinete
Celery - Țelină
Spinach - Spanac
Beans – Fasole
Corn - Porumb
Artichoke - Anghinare
Tomato - Roșie/ **Carrot** - Morcov/ **Lettuce** - Salată verde
Radish - Ridiche / **Beet** - Sfeclă/ **Chard** - Sfeclă roșie
Bell Pepper – Ardei Gras/ **Hot pepper** – Ardei iute
Garlic - Usturoi/ **Onion** - Ceapa
Cabbage - Varză/ **Cauliflower** - Conopida
Grilled vegetables – Legume la grătar
Steamed vegetables – Legume fierte la abur

Grilled vegetables or steamed vegetables are popular side dishes at restaurants.
Legumele la grătar sau legumele la abur sunt garnituri populare în restaurante.
There are carrots, bell peppers, lettuce, and radishes in my salad.
În salata mea sunt morcovi, ardei gras, salată verde și ridichi.
It's not hard to grow tomatoes.
Nu este greu să cultivi roșii.
Eggplant can be cooked or fried.
Vinetele pot fi gătite sau prăjite.
I like beets in my salad.
Îmi place sfecla în salată.
I don't like to eat hot peppers.
Nu-mi place să mănânc ardei iute.
Celery and spinach have natural vitamins.
Țelina și spanacul au vitamine naturale.
Fried cauliflower tastes better than fried cabbage.
Conopida prăjită are un gust mai bun decât varza prăjită.
Rice and beans are my favorite side dish.
Orezul și fasolea sunt garnitura mea preferată.
I like butter on corn.
Îmi place untul pe porumb.
Garlic is an important ingredient in many cuisines.
Usturoiul este un ingredient important în multe bucătării.
Where is the onion powder?
Unde este praful de ceapa?
An artichoke is difficult to peel.
O anghinare este dificil de curățat.

Cucumber – Castraveți
Lentils - Linte / **Peas -** Mazăre
Green onion – Ceapa verde
Herbs - Ierburi / **Basil -** Busuioc
Parsley - Pătrunjel/ **Cilantro -** Coriandru
Dill - Mărar/ **Mint -** Mentă
Potato – Cartofi/ **Sweet Potato -** Cartofi dulci
Mushroom – Ciupercă / **Asparagus -** Sparanghel
Pumpkin – Dovleac / **Squash -** Kürbis / **Zucchini -** Dovlecel
Chick peas – Năut
Seaweed – Alge marine
Vegetable garden – Gradina de legume

I want to order lentil soup.
Vreau să comand supă de linte.
Please put the green onion in the refrigerator.
Vă rugăm să puneți ceapa verde la frigider.
The most common kitchen herbs are basil, cilantro, dill, parsley, and mint.
Cele mai comune ierburi de bucătărie sunt busuiocul, coriandrul, mărarul, pătrunjelul și menta.
Some of the most common vegetables for tempura are sweet potatoes and mushrooms.
Unele dintre cele mai frecvente legume pentru tempura sunt cartofii dulci și ciupercile.
I want to order vegetarian sushi with asparagus and cucumber along with a side of seaweed salad.
Vreau să comand sushi vegetarian cu sparanghel și castraveți împreună cu o garnitură de salată de alge marine.
I enjoy eating pumpkin seeds as a snack.
Îmi face plăcere să mănânc semințe de dovleac ca gustare.
I must water my vegetable garden.
Trebuie să-mi ud grădina de legume.
The potatoes in the field are ready to harvest.
Cartofii din câmp sunt gata de recoltare.
Chickpeas are a popular ingredient in Middle Eastern food.
Năutul este un ingredient popular în mâncarea din Orientul Mijlociu.
Is there Zucchini in the soup?
Există dovlecel în supă?
I like to put ginger dressing on my salad.
Îmi place să pun dressing de ghimbir pe salată.
The tomatoes are fresh but the cucumbers are rotten.
Roșiile sunt proaspete, dar castraveții sunt putrezi.

FRUITS - FRUCTE

Apple - Măr
Banana - Banana
Orange - Portocală/ **Grapefruit** - Grapefruituri
Peach - Piersică
Tropical fruit - Fruct tropical
Papaya - Papaya / **Coconut** - Nucă de cocos
Cherry - Cireş
Raisins - Stafide/ **Prune** - Prună
Dates - Curmale / **Fig** - Smochine
Fruit salad - Salată de fructe/ **Dried fruit** - Fructe uscate
Apricot - Caise/ **Pear** - Pară
Avocado - Avocado / **Ripe** – Coaptă /maturată

Can I add raisins to the apple pie?
Pot adăuga stafide la plăcinta cu mere?
Orange juice is a wonderful source of Vitamin C.
Sucul de portocale este o sursă minunată de vitamina C.
Grapefruits are extremely beneficial for your health.
Grapefruiturile sunt extrem de benefice pentru sănătatea ta.
I have a peach tree in my front yard
Am un piersic în curtea din faţă
I bought papayas and coconuts at the supermarket to prepare a fruit salad.
Am cumpărat papaya şi nuci de cocos de la supermarket pentru a pregăti o salată de fructe.
I want to travel to Japan to see the famous cherry blossom.
Vreau să călătoresc în Japonia pentru a vedea celebra floare de cireş.
Bananas are tropical fruits.
Bananele sunt fructe tropicale.
I want to mix dates and figs in my fruit salad.
Vreau să amestec curmale şi smochine în salata mea de fructe.
Apricots and prunes are my favorite dried fruits.
Caisele şi prunele uscate sunt fructele mele uscate preferate.
Pears are delicious.
Perele sunt delicioase.
The avocado isn't ripe yet.
Avocado nu este încă copt.
The green apple is very sour.
Mărul verde este foarte acru.
The unripe peach is usually bitter.
Piersica necoaptă este de obicei amară.

Fruit tree - Pom fructifer
Citrus - Citrice
Lemon - Lămâie
Lime - Lămâie verde
Pineapple - Ananas
Melon - Pepene galben
Watermelon - Pepene verde
Strawberry - Căpşună
Berry - coacăză
Blueberry - Afină
Raspberry - Zmeură
Grapes - Struguri
Pomegranate - Rodie
Plum - Prună
Olive - Măslină
Grove - Crâng

Strawberries grow during the Spring.
Căpşunile cresc în timpul primăverii.
How much does the watermelon juice cost?
Cât costă sucul de pepene verde?
I have a pineapple plant in a pot.
Am o plantă de ananas într-o oală.
Melons grow on the ground.
Pepenii cresc pe pământ.
I am going to the fruit-tree section of the nursery today to purchase a few citrus trees.
Mă duc astăzi la secţiunea de pomi fructiferi din pepinieră pentru a cumpăra câţiva pomi de citrice.
There are many raspberries growing on the bush.
Pe tufiş creşte multă zmeură.
Blueberry juice is very sweet.
Sucul de afine este foarte dulce.
I need to pick the grapes to make the wine.
Trebuie să culeg strugurii pentru a face vinul.
Pomegranate juice contains a very high level of antioxidants.
Sucul de rodie conţine un nivel foarte ridicat de antioxidanţi.
Plums are seasonal fruits.
Prunele sunt fructe de sezon.
I add either lemon juice or lime juice to my salad.
Adaug fie suc de lamaie, fie suc de limetă in salata mea.
I have an olive grove in my backyard.
Am o livadă de măslini în curtea din spate.

SHOPPING - CUMPĂRĂTURI

Clothes - Haine
Clothing store - Magazin de îmbrăcăminte
For sale - De vânzare
Hat - Pălărie
Shirt - Cămașă
Shoes - Pantofi
Skirt - Fustă/ **Dress** - Rochie
Pants - Pantaloni
Shorts - Pantaloni scurti
Suit - Costum/ **Vest** - Vestă
Tie - Cravată
Uniform - Uniformă
Belt - Centură
Socks - Șosete
Gloves - Mănuși
Glasses - Ochelari/ **Sunglasses** - Ochelari de soare
Size - Dimensiune
Small - Mic/ **Medium** - Mediu/ **Large** - Mare/ **Thick** - Gros/ **Thin** - Subțire
Thrift store - Magazin second-hand

There are a lot of clothes for sale today.
Sunt o mulțime de haine de vânzare astăzi.
Does this hat look good?
Arată bine această pălărie?
I am happy with this shirt and these shoes.
Sunt mulțumit de această cămașă și de acești pantofi.
She prefers a skirt instead of a dress.
Ea preferă o fustă în loc de rochie.
These pants aren't my size.
Acesti pantaloni nu sunt marimea mea.
Where can I find a thrift store? I want to buy a suit, a vest, and a tie.
Unde pot găsi un magazin second-hand? Vreau să-mi cumpăr un costum, o vestă și o cravată.
There are uniforms for school at the clothing store.
Există uniforme pentru școală la magazinul de îmbrăcăminte.
I forgot my socks, belt, and shorts at your house.
Mi-am uitat șosetele, cureaua și pantalonii scurți la tine acasă.
These gloves are a size too small. Do you have a medium size?
Aceste mănuși au o dimensiune prea mică. Ai o dimensiune medie?
Today I don't need my reading glasses. However, I have my sunglasses.
Astăzi nu am nevoie de ochelarii mei de citit. Oricum, am ochelarii de soare.

Jacket - Geacă
Scarf - Eşarfă
Mittens - Mănuşi
Sleeve - Mânecă
Boots (rain, winter) – Cizme (**ploaie, iarnă**)
Sweater - Pulover
Bathing suit - Costum de baie
Flip flops - Şlapi
Tank top - Bluză de corp
Sandals - Sandale
Heels - Tocuri
On sale - La reducere
Expensive - Scump
Free - Gratuit**/ Discount -** Reducere**/ Cheap -** Ieftin
Shopping - Cumpărături / **Mall -** Mall

We are going to the mountain today so don't forget your jacket, mittens, and scarf.
Azi mergem la munte, aşa că nu uitaţi de geacă, mănuşi şi fular.
I have long sleeve shirts and short sleeve shirts.
Am cămăși cu mânecă lungă și cămăși cu mânecă scurtă.
Boots and sweaters are meant for winter.
Cizmele și puloverele sunt pentru iarnă.
At the beach, I wear a bathing suit and flip flops.
La plajă, port costum de baie şi şlapi.
I want to buy a tank top for summer.
Vreau să cumpăr un top pentru vară.
I can't wear heels on the beach, only sandals.
Nu pot purta tocuri pe plajă, doar sandale.
What will be on sale tomorrow?
Ce va fi la reduceri mâine?
This is free.
Acest lucru este gratuit.
Even though this cologne and this perfume are discounted, they are still very expensive.
Chiar dacă această apă de toaletă și acest parfum sunt la preț redus, ele sunt totuși foarte scumpe.
These items are very cheap.
Aceste articole sunt foarte ieftine.
I can go shopping only on weekends.
Pot să merg la cumpărături doar în weekend.
Is the local mall far?
Mall-ul local este departe?

Store - Magazin
Business hours - Programul de lucru
Open - Deschis / **Closed -** Închis
Entrance - Intrare/ **Exit -** Ieşire
Shopping cart - Cărucior de cumpărături
Shopping basket - Coş de cumpărături
Shopping bag - Geantă de cumpărături
Toy store - Magazin de jucării / **Toy -** Jucărie
Book store - Librărie / **Music store -** Magazin de muzică
Jeweler - Bijutier/ **Jewelry -** Bijuterii
Gold - Aur/ **Silver -** Argint
Necklace - Colier/ **Bracelet –** Brăţară/ **Diamond -** Diamant
Gift - Cadou
Coin - Monedă
Antique - Antic
Dealer - Comerciant

What are your (plural) **business hours?**
Care sunt orele tale de lucru (la plural)?
What time does the store open?
La ce oră se deschide magazinul?
What times does the store close?
La ce oră se închide magazinul?
Where is the entrance?
Unde este intrarea?
Where is the exit?
Unde este ieşirea?
My children want to go to the toy store so they can fill up the shopping cart with toys.
Copiii mei vor să meargă la magazinul de jucării ca să poată umple coşul de cumpărături cu jucării.
I use a large shopping basket at the supermarket.
Folosesc un coş mare de cumpărături la supermarket.
There is a sale at the bookstore right now.
Există o reducere la librărie chiar acum.
The jeweler sells gold and silver.
Bijutierul vinde aur şi argint.
I want to buy a diamond necklace.
Vreau să cumpăr un colier cu diamante.
This bracelet and those pair of earrings are gifts for my daughter.
Această brăţară şi acele perechi de cercei sunt cadouri pentru fiica mea.
He is an antique coin dealer.
Este un comerciant de monede antice.

FAMILY - FAMILIE

Mother - Mamă
Father - Tată
Son - Fiu/ **Daughter -** Fiică
Brother - Frate
Sister - Soră
Husband - Soț
Wife - Soție
Parent - Părinte**/ Parents** (plural) **-** Părinți
Child - Copil
Baby - Bebeluș
Grandfather - Bunic
Grandmother – Bunică
Grandparents - Bunici
Grandson - Nepot
Granddaughter - Nepoată
Grandchildren - Nepoți
Nephew - Nepot/ **Niece -** Nepoată
Cousin - Văr

I have a big family.
Am o familie mare.
My brother and sister are here.
Fratele și sora mea sunt aici.
The mother and father want to spend time with their child.
Mama și tatăl vor să petreacă timp cu copilul lor.
He wants to bring his son and daughter to the public park.
Vrea să-și aducă fiul și fiica în parcul public.
The grandfather wants to take his grandson to the movie.
Bunicul vrea să-și ducă nepotul la film.
The grandmother wants to give her granddaughter money.
Bunica vrea să-i dea bani nepoatei sale.
The grandparents want to spend time with their grandchildren.
Bunicii vor să petreacă timp cu nepoții lor.
The husband and wife have a new baby.
Soțul și soția au un nou copil.
I want to go to the park with my niece and nephew.
Vreau să merg în parc cu nepoata și nepotul meu.
My cousin wants to see his children.
Vărul meu vrea să-și vadă copiii.
That man is a good parent.
Omul acela este un părinte bun.

Aunt - Mătuşă / **Uncle -** Unchi
Man - Om/ **Woman -** Femeie
Stepfather - Tată vitreg/ **Stepmother -** Mamă vitregă
Stepbrother - Frate vitreg/ **Stepsister -** Sora vitregă
Stepson - Fiu vitreg/ **Stepdaughter -** Fiica vitregă
In-laws - Socri
Ancestors - Strămoşi
Family tree - Arborele genealogic
Generation - Generaţie
First born - Primul născut/ **Only child -** Unicul copil
Relative - Rudă/ **Family member -** Membru al familiei
Twins - Gemeni
Pregnant - Insarcinată
Adopted child - Copil adoptat
Orphan - Orfan
Adult - Adult
Neighbor - Vecin/ **Friend -** Prieten
Roommate - Coleg de cameră

My aunt and uncle came here for a visit.
Mătuşa şi unchiul meu au venit aici în vizită.
He is their only child.
El este singurul lor copil.
My wife is pregnant with twins.
Soţia mea este însărcinată cu gemeni.
He is their eldest son.
El este fiul lor cel mare.
The first-born child usually takes on all the responsibilities.
Primul născut îşi asumă de obicei toate responsabilităţile.
I was able to find all my relatives and ancestors on my family tree.
Am reuşit să-mi găsesc toate rudele şi strămoşii în arborele meu genealogic.
My parents' generation loved disco music.
Generaţia părinţilor mei iubea muzica disco.
Their adopted child was an orphan
Copilul lor adoptat a fost orfan
I like my in-laws.
Îmi plac socrii mei.
I have a nice neighbor.
Am un vecin drăguţ.
She considers her stepson as her real son.
Îşi consideră fiul vitreg drept fiul ei natural.
She is his stepdaughter.
Ea este fiica lui vitregă.

HUMAN BODY - CORPUL UMAN

Head - Cap
Face - Față
Eye - Ochi/ **(p)** ochi**, Ear** - Ureche/ **(p)** urechi
Nose - Nas
Mouth - Gură/ **Lips** - Buze
Tongue - Limbă
Cheek - Obraz
Chin - Chin
Neck - Gât/ **Throat** - Gât
Forehead - Frunte
Eyebrow - Spranceană/ **Eyelashes** - Gene
Hair - Păr/ **Beard** - Barbă/ **Mustache** - Mustață
Tooth - Dinte/ **(p)** dinți

My chin, cheeks, mouth, lips, and eyes are all part of my face.
Bărbia, obrajii, gura, buzele și ochii fac parte din fața mea.
He has small ears.
El are urechi mici.
I have a cold so therefore my nose, eyes, mouth, and tongue are affected.
Sunt răcit, așa că îmi sunt afectate nasul, ochii, gura și limba.
The five senses are sight, touch, taste, smell, and hearing.
Cele cinci simțuri sunt văzul, atingerea, gustul, mirosul și auzul.
I am washing my face right now.
Mă spăl pe față chiar acum.
I have a headache
Mă doare capul.
My eyebrows are too long.
Sprâncenele mele sunt prea lungi.
He must shave his beard and mustache.
Trebuie să-și radă barba și mustața.
I brush my teeth every morning.
Mă spăl pe dinți în fiecare dimineață.
She puts makeup on her cheeks and a lot of lipstick on her lips.
Își machiază obrajii și își pune mult ruj pe buze.
Her hair covered her forehead.
Părul îi acoperea fruntea.
She has a long neck.
Ea are gâtul lung.
I have a sore throat.
Am o durere în gât.

Shoulder - Umăr
Chest - Piept
Arm - Braț
Hand - Mână**/ Palm** (of hand) – Palmă (a mâinii)
Elbow - Cot**/ Wrist -** Încheietura mâinii
Finger - Deget**/ Thumb -** Degetul mare
Back - Înapoi
Belly - Burtă/ **Stomach -** Stomac/ **Intestines -** Intestine
Brain - Creier/ **Heart -** Inimă**/ Kidneys -** Rinichi
Lungs - Plămânii **/ Liver -** Ficat
Leg - Picior/ **Ankle -** Gleznă
Foot - Picior**/ Palm** (of foot) – Laba piciorului
Toe – Deget de la picior **/ Nail -** Unghie
Joint - Articulație **/ Muscle -** Muschi
Spine - Coloana vertebrală **/Skeleton -** Schelet
Bone - os **/Ribs -** Coaste**/Skull -** Craniu
Skin - Piele **/ Vein -** Venă

He has a problem with his stomach.
Are o problemă cu stomacul.
The brain, heart, kidneys, lungs, and liver are internal organs.
Creierul, inima, rinichii, plămânii și ficatul sunt organe interne.
His chest and shoulders are very muscular.
Pieptul și umerii îi sunt foarte musculoși.
I need to strengthen my arms and legs.
Trebuie să-mi întăresc brațele și picioarele.
I accidentally hit his wrist with my elbow.
L-am lovit din greșeală încheietura mâinii cu cotul.
I have pain in every part of my body especially in my hand, ankle, and back.
Am dureri în fiecare parte a corpului, în special în mână, gleznă și spate.
I want to cut my nails.
Vreau să-mi tai unghiile.
I need a new bandage for my thumb.
Am nevoie de un bandaj nou pentru degetul mare.
I have a cast on my foot because of a broken bone.
Am un ghips la picior din cauza unui os rupt.
I have muscles and joint pain today.
Am dureri de mușchi și articulații astăzi.
The spine is the main part of the body.
Coloana vertebrală este partea principală a corpului.
I have beautiful skin.
Am o piele frumoasă.

HEALTH AND MEDICAL - SĂNĂTATE ŞI MEDICAL

Disease - Boală
Bacteria - Bacterii
Sick - Bolnav
Clinic - Clinică
Headache - Durere de cap / **Earache** - Durere de urechi
Pharmacy - Farmacie/ **Prescription** - Prescripție medicală
Symptoms - Simptome
Nausea - Greață/ **Stomachache** - Durere de stomac
Allergy - Alergie
Penicillin - Penicilină/ **Antibiotic** - Antibiotic
Sore throat - Durere în gât / **Fever** - Febră/ **Flu** - Gripă
Cough - Tuse/ **To cough** - A tuşi
Infection - Infecție/ **Injury** - Accident/ **Scar** - Cicatrice
Ache / pain - Durere
Intensive care - Terapie intensivă
Bandaid - Bandaj/ **Bandage** - Pansament

Are you in good health?
Esti sanatos?
These bacteria caused this disease.
Aceste bacterii au cauzat această boală.
He is very sick.
El este foarte bolnav.
I have a headache so I must go to the pharmacy to refill my prescription.
Mă doare capul aşa că trebuie să merg la farmacie să-mi refac rețeta.
The main symptoms of food poisoning are nausea and stomach ache.
Principalele simptome ale intoxicațiilor alimentare sunt greața şi durerile de stomac.
I have an allergy to penicillin, so I need another antibiotic.
Am o alergie la penicilină, asa ca am nevoie de un alt antibiotic.
What do I need to treat an earache?
De ce am nevoie pentru a trata o durere de urechi?
I need to go to the clinic for my fever and sore throat.
Trebuie să merg la clinică pentru febră şi durere în gât.
The bandage won't help your infection.
Bandajul nu te va ajuta cu infecția.
I have a serious injury so I must go to intensive care.
Am o accidentare gravă, aşa că trebuie să merg la terapie intensivă.
I have muscle and joint pains today.
Azi am dureri musculare şi articulare.

Hospital - Spital
Doctor - Doctor, medic / **Nurse -** Asistentă
Family Doctor - Medic de familie / **Pediatrician -** Pediatru
Medication - Medicament/ **Pills -** Pastile
Heartburn - Arsuri gastrice
Paramedic – Asistent medical/ **Emergency room -** Camera de urgență
Health insurance - Asigurare de sănătate / **Patient -** Pacient
Surgery - Chirurgie/ **Surgeon -** Chirurg / **Face mask -** Mască facială
Anesthesia - Anestezie / **Local anesthesia -** Anestezie locală
General anesthesia - Anestezie generală
Wheelchair - Scaun cu rotile/ **Cane –** Baston
Walker – Suport de mers / **Stretcher -** Targă
Dialysis - Dializă/ **Insulin -** Insulină/ **Diabetes** - Diabet
Temperature - Temperatură/ **Thermometer -** Termometru
A shot - O lovitură / **Needle -** Ac/ **Syringe -** Seringă
In need of - Am nevoie de

Where is the closest hospital?
Unde este cel mai apropiat spital?
Usually we see the nurse before the doctor.
De obicei, vedem asistenta înaintea medicului.
The paramedics can take her to the emergency room but she doesn't have health insurance.
Paramedicii o pot duce la camera de urgență, dar nu are asigurare de sănătate.
The doctor treated the patient.
Medicul a tratat pacientul.
He needs knee surgery today.
Are nevoie de o operație la genunchi astăzi.
The surgeon needs to administer general anesthesia in order to operate on the patient.
Chirurgul trebuie să administreze anestezie generală pentru a opera pacientul.
Does the patient need a wheelchair or a stretcher?
Pacientul are nevoie de scaun cu rotile sau targă?
I have to take medicine every day.
Trebuie să iau medicamente în fiecare zi.
Do you have any pills for heartburn?
Ai pastile pentru arsuri la stomac?
Where is the closest dialysis center?
Unde este cel mai apropiat centru de dializă?
The doctor didn't prescribe insulin for my diabetes.
Doctorul nu mi-a prescris insulină pentru diabetul meu.
I need a thermometer to take my temperature.
Am nevoie de un termometru pentru a-mi lua temperatura.

Stroke - Accident vascular cerebral
Blood - Sânge**/ Blood pressure -** Tensiune arterială
Heart attack - Infarct
Cancer - Cancer**/ Chemotherapy -** Chimioterapie
Help - Ajutor
Germs - Germeni **/ Virus -** Virus
Vaccine - Vaccin**/ A cure -** Un leac / **To cure -** A vindeca
Cholesterol - Colesterol**/ Nutrition -** Nutriție**/ Diet -** Dieta
Blind - Orb**/ Deaf -** Surd**/ Mute -** Mut
Young - Tânăr **/ Elderly -** Vârstnici
Fat - Gras / **Skinny** (person) – Slab (persoană)
Nursing home - Azil de bătrâni
Disability, handicap - Handicap**/ Paralysis -** Paralizie
Depression - Depresie**/ Anxiety -** Anxietate
Dentist - Stomatolog / **X-ray -** Raze X
Tooth cavity - Carie dentară
Tooth paste - Pastă de dinți **/ Tooth brush -** Periuță de dinți

A stroke is caused by a lack of blood flow to the brain.
Un accident vascular cerebral este cauzat de lipsa fluxului sangvin către creier.
These are the symptoms of a heart attack.
Acestea sunt simptomele unui atac de cord.
Chemotherapy is for treating cancer.
Chimioterapia este pentru tratarea cancerului.
Proper nutrition is very important and you must avoid foods that are high in cholesterol.
Alimentația corectă este foarte importantă și trebuie să evitați alimentele bogate în colesterol.
I am starting my diet today.
Azi incep dieta.
There is no cure for this virus, only a vaccine.
Nu există leac pentru acest virus, doar un vaccin.
The nursing home is open 365 days a year.
Azilul de bătrâni este deschis 365 de zile pe an.
I don't like suffering from depression and anxiety.
Nu-mi place să sufer de depresie și anxietate.
Soap and water kill germs.
Apa și săpunul ucid germenii.
The dentist took X-rays of my teeth to check for cavities.
Medicul dentist mi-a făcut radiografii ale dinților pentru a verifica dacă există carii.
In the morning I put tooth paste on my toothbrush.
Dimineață am pus pastă de dinți pe periuța de dinți.

EMERGENCY & DISASTERS - URGENȚĂ ȘI DEZASTRE

Help - Ajutor
Fire - Foc
Ambulance - Ambulanță
First aid - Primul ajutor
CPR – CPR (RCP)
Emergency number - Număr de urgență
Accident - Accident/ **Car crash -** Accident de mașină
Death - Moarte**/ Deadly -** Mortal/ **Fatality -** Deces
Lightly wounded - Ușor rănit
Moderately wounded - Rănit moderat
Seriously wounded - Grav rănit
Fire truck - Camion de pompieri **/ Siren -** Sirena
Fire extinguisher - Extinctor
Police - Politie**/ Police station -** Secția de poliție
Robbery - Jaf **/ Thief -** Hoț**/ Murderer -** Ucigaș

There is a fire. I need to call for help.
Există un incendiu. Trebuie să chem pentru ajutor.
I need to call an ambulance.
Trebuie să chem o ambulanță.
That accident was bad.
Accidentul acela a fost rău.
The thief wants to steal my money.
Hoțul vrea să-mi fure banii.
The car crash was fatal, there were two deaths, and four suffered serious injuries.
Accidentul a fost fatal, s-au înregistrat doi morți, iar patru au suferit răni grave.
One was moderately wounded and two were lightly wounded.
Unul a fost rănit moderat și doi au fost răniți ușor.
CPR is a first step of first-aid.
RCP este un prim pas al primului ajutor.
Please provide me with the emergency number.
Vă rog să-mi furnizați numărul de urgență.
The police are on their way.
Poliția este pe drum.
I must call the police station to report a robbery.
Trebuie să sun la secția de poliție să raportez un jaf.
The siren of the fire truck is very loud.
Sirena mașinii de pompieri sună foarte tare.
Where is the fire extinguisher?
Unde este extinctorul?

Fire hydrant - Hidrant de incendiu
Fireman - Pompier
Emergency situation - Situație de urgență
Explosion - Explozie
Rescue - Salvare
Natural disaster - Dezastru natural
Destruction - Distrugere
Damage - Daune
Hurricane - Uragan **/ Tornado -** Tornadă
Flood - Inundație **/ Overflow** (water) **–** Revărsare (a apei)
Storm – Furtună
Snowstorm - Furtună de zăpadă
Hail - Grindină
Bomb shelter - Adăpost antibombă
Refuge - Refugiu
Cause - Cauză
Safety - Siguranță
Drought - Secetă**/ Famine -** Foamete
Poverty - Sărăcia
Epidemic - Epidemie**/ Pandemic -** Pandemie

It's prohibited to park by the fire hydrant in case of a fire.
Este interzisă parcarea lângă hidrantul de incendiu în caz de incendiu.
When there is a fire, the first to arrive on scene are the firemen.
Când are loc un incendiu, primii care vin la fața locului sunt pompierii.
There is a fire. I must call for help.
Există un incendiu. Trebuie să chem ajutor.
In an emergency situation everyone needs to be rescued.
Într-o situație de urgență, toți trebuie să fie salvați.
The gas explosion led to a natural disaster.
Explozia de gaz a dus la un dezastru natural.
During a siren you need to run to the bomb shelter.
Când sună o sirenă, trebuie să fugi la adăpostul anti-bombe.
The hurricane caused a lot of damage and destruction in its path.
Uraganul a provocat multe pagube și distrugeri în calea sa.
The tornado destroyed the town.
Tornada a distrus orașul.
The drought led to famine and a lot of poverty.
Seceta a dus la foamete și multă sărăcie.
There were three days of flooding following the storm.
Au fost trei zile de inundații în urma furtunii.
This is a snowstorm and not a hail storm.
Aceasta este o furtună de zăpadă și nu o furtună de grindină.

Danger - Pericol
Dangerous - Periculos
A warning - Un avertisment
Warning! - Avertizare!!
Earthquake - Cutremur
Disaster - Dezastru
Disaster area - Zona dezastrelor
Mandatory - Obligatoriu
Evacuation - Evacuare
Safe place - Loc sigur
Blackout – Pană de curent
Rainstorm - Furtună de ploaie
Avalanche - Avalanșă
Heatwave - Caniculă
Rip current – Curent puternic
Tsunami - Tsunami
Whirlpool - Furtună
Lightning - Fulger
Thunder - Tunet

We need to stay in a safe place during the earthquake.
Trebuie să stăm într-un loc sigur în timpul cutremurului.
Heatwaves are usually in the summer.
Valurile de căldură sunt de obicei vara.
This is a disaster area, therefore there is a mandatory evacuation order.
Aceasta este o zonă de dezastru, prin urmare există un ordin de evacuare obligatoriu.
There was a blackout for three hours due to the rainstorm.
A fost o întrerupere de current timp de trei ore din cauza furtunii.
Be careful during the snowstorm, because there might be an avalanche.
Atenție în timpul furtunii de zăpadă, pentru că ar putea fi o avalanșă.
There is a tsunami warning today.
Astăzi există o avertizare de tsunami.
You can't swim against a rip current.
Nu poți înota împotriva unui curent puternic.
There is a dangerous whirlpool in the ocean.
Există un vârtej periculos în ocean.
There is a risk of lightning today.
Există riscul de fulger astăzi.

HOME - ACASĂ

Living room - Camera de zi
Living room - Sufragerie
Couch - Canapea
Sofa - Divan
Door - Ușă
Closet - Dulap
Stairway - Scară
Rug - Covor
Curtain - Perdea
Window - Fereastră
Floor - Podea
Floor (as in level) – Etaj
Fireplace - Șemineu / **Chimney** - Horn
Candle - Lumânare
Laundry detergent - Detergent de rufe
Pantry - Cămară
Toothpicks - Scobitori

The living room is missing a couch and a sofa.
În sufragerie lipsește o canapea și un divan.
I must buy a new door for my closet.
Trebuie să cumpăr o ușă nouă pentru dulapul meu.
The spiral staircase is beautiful.
Scara în spirală este frumoasă.
There aren't any curtains on the windows.
Nu există perdele la ferestre.
I have a marble floor on the first floor and a wooden floor on the second floor.
Am o podea de marmură la primul etaj și o podea de lemn la etajul doi.
I can only light this candle now.
Nu pot să aprind această lumânare decât acum.
The fire sparkles in the fireplace.
Focul scoate scântei în șemineu.
I can clean the floors today and then I want to arrange the closet.
Pot curăța podelele azi și apoi vreau să aranjez dulapul.
I have to wash the rug with laundry detergent.
Trebuie să spăl covorul cu detergent de rufe.
There is canned food in the pantry.
Există conserve în cămară.
Where are the toothpicks?
Unde sunt scobitorile?

Silverware - Argintărie
Knife - Cuțit
Spoon – Lingură
Fork - Furculiță
Teaspoon - Linguriță
Kitchen - Bucătărie
A cup - O ceașcă
A mug - O cană
Plate - Farfurie
Bowl - Bol
Little bowl - Castron mic
Napkin - Șervețel
Table - masă
Placemat - Covoraș de masă
Table cloth - Față de masă
Glass (material) - Sticlă
A glass (cup) - Un pahar
Oven - Cuptor
Stove - Aragaz
Pot (cooking) - Oală
Pan - Pan
Cabinet - Dulap
Drawer - Sertar

The knives, spoons, teaspoons, and forks are inside the drawer in the kitchen.
Cuțitele, lingurile, lingurițele și furculițele sunt în interiorul sertarului din bucătărie.
There aren't enough cups, plates, and silverware on the table for everyone.
Nu sunt suficiente cești, farfurii și argintărie pe masă pentru toată lumea.
The napkin is underneath the bowl.
Șervețelul este sub vas.
The placemats are on the table.
Covorașele sunt pe masă.
The table cloth is beautiful.
Fața de masă este frumoasă.
The pizza is in the oven.
Pizza este la cuptor.
The pots and pans are in the cabinet.
Oalele și tigăile sunt în dulap.
The stove isn't functioning.
Aragazul nu funcționează.

Bedroom - Dormitor
Bed - Pat
Mattress - Saltea
Blanket - Pătură
Bed sheet - Cearceaf de pat
Pillow - Pernă
Mirror - Oglindă
Chair - Scaun
Dining room - Sala de mese
Hallway - Hol
Downstairs – La parter
Towel - Prosop
Bathroom - Baie
Bathtub - Cada de baie
Shower - Duș
Sink - Chiuvetă
Faucet - Robinet
Soap - Săpun
Box - Cutie

The master bedroom is at the end of the hallway, and the dining room is downstairs.
Dormitorul matrimonial este la capătul holului, iar sufrageria este la parter.
The mirror looks good in the bedroom.
Oglinda arată bine în dormitor.
I have to buy a new bed and a new mattress.
Trebuie să cumpăr un pat nou și o saltea nouă.
Where are the blankets and bed sheets?
Unde sunt păturile și cearșafurile de pat?
My pillows are on the chair.
Pernele mele sunt pe scaun.
These towels are for drying your hand.
Aceste prosoape sunt pentru uscarea mâinilor.
The bathtub, shower, and the sink are old.
Cada, dușul și chiuveta sunt vechi.
I need soap to wash my hands.
Am nevoie de săpun să mă spăl pe mâini.
The guest bathroom is in the corner of the hallway.
Baia de oaspeți este în colțul holului.
How many boxes does he have?
El câte cutii are?

Room - Cameră
Balcony - Balcon
Shelve - Raft
Roof - Acoperiş
Ceiling - Tavan
Wall - Perete
Carpet - Covor
Attic - Mansardă
Basement - Subsol
Trash - Gunoi
Garbage can - Coş de gunoi
Driveway – Drum de acces
Garden - Grădină
Backyard - Curtea din spate
Jar - Borcan
Doormat - Preş
Bag - Geantă
Key - Cheie

I can install new windows for my balcony.
Îmi pot instala ferestre noi pentru balcon.
I must install a new roof.
Trebuie să montez un acoperiş nou.
The color of my ceiling is white.
Culoarea tavanului meu este albă.
I must paint the walls.
Trebuie să pictez pereţii.
The attic is an extra room in the house.
Mansarda este o cameră suplimentară în casă.
The kids are playing either in the basement or the backyard.
Copiii se joacă fie în subsol, fie în curtea din spate.
All the glass jars are outside on the doormat.
Toate borcanele de sticlă sunt afară, pe preş.
The garbage can is blocking the driveway.
Coşul de gunoi blochează drumul de acces.
The glasses on the shelve are used for champagne, not wine.
Paharele de pe raft sunt folosite pentru şampanie, nu pentru vin.
I want to put my things in the plastic bag.
Vreau să-mi pun lucrurile în punga de plastic.
I need to bring my keys.
Trebuie să-mi aduc cheile.
All the photographs are in the attic.
Toate fotografiile sunt în mansardă.

Conclusion

You have now learned a wide range of sentences in relation to a variety of topics such as the home and garden. You can discuss the roof and ceiling of a house, plus natural disasters like hurricanes and thunderstorms.

The combination of sentences can also work well when caught in a natural disaster and having to deal with emergency issues. When the electricity gets cut you can tell your family or friends, "I can only light this candle now." As you're running out of the house, remind yourself of the essentials by saying, "I need to bring my keys with me."

If you need to go to a hospital, you have now been provided with sentences and the vocabulary for talking to doctors and nurses and dealing with surgery and health issues. Most importantly, you can ask, "What is the emergency number in this country?" When you get to the hospital, tell the health services, "The hurricane caused a lot of destruction and damage in its path," and "We used the hurricane shelter for refuge."

The three hundred and fifty words that you learned in part 1 should have been a big help to you with these new themes. When learning the Romanian language, you are now more able to engage with people in Romanian, which should make your travels flow a lot easier.

Part 3 will introduce you to additional topics that will be invaluable to your journeys. You will learn vocabulary in relation to politics, the military, and the family. The three books in this series all together provide a flawless system of learning the Romanian language. When you visit Romania, you will now have the capacity for greater conversational learning.

When you proceed to Part 3 you will be able to expand your vocabulary and conversational skills even further. Your range of topics will expand to the office environment, business negotiations and even school.

Please, feel free to post a review in order to share your experience or suggest feedback as to how this method can be improved.

Conversational Romanian Quick and Easy

The Most Innovative Technique to Learn the Romanian Language

Part III

YATIR NITZANY

Introduction to the Program

You have now reached Part 3 of Conversational Romanian Quick and Easy. In Part 1 you learned the 350 words that could be used in an infinite number of combinations. In Part 2 you moved on to putting these words into sentences. You learned how to ask for help when your house was hit by a hurricane and how to find the emergency services. For example, if you need to go to a hospital, you have now been provided with sentences and the vocabulary for talking to doctors and nurses and dealing with surgery and health issues. When you get to the hospital, you can tell the health services, "The hurricane caused a lot of destruction and damage in its path," and "We used the hurricane shelter for refuge."

In this third book in the series, you will find the culmination of this foreign language course that is based on a system using key phrases used in day-to-day life. You can now move on to further topics such as things you would say in an office. This theme is ideal if you've just moved to Romanian for a new job. You may be about to sit at your desk to do an important task assigned to you by your boss but you have forgotten the details you were given. Turn to your colleagues and say, "I have to write an important email but I forgot my password." Then, if the reply is "Our secretary isn't here today. Only the receptionist is here but she is in the bathroom," you'll know what is being said and you can wait for help. By the end of the first few weeks, you'll have at your disposal terminology that can help reflect your experiences. "I want to retire already," you may find yourself saying at coffee break on a Monday morning after having had to go to your bank manager and say, "I need a small loan in order to pay my mortgage this month."

I came up with the idea of this unique system of learning foreign languages as I was struggling with my own attempt to learn Romanian. When playing around with word combinations I discovered 350 words that when used together could make up an infinite number of sentences. From this beginning,

I was able to start speaking in a new language. I then practiced and found that I could use the same technique with other languages, such as Spanish, French, Italian and Arabic. It was a revelation.

This method is by far the easiest and quickest way to master other languages and begin practicing conversational language skills.

The range of topics and the core vocabulary are the main components of this flawless learning method. In Part 3 you have a chance to learn how to relate to people in many more ways. Sports, for example, are very important for keeping healthy and in good spirits. The social component of these types of activities should not be underestimated at all. You will, therefore, have much help when you meet some new people, perhaps in a bar, and want to say to them, "I like to watch basketball games," and "Today are the finals of the Olympic Games. Let's see who wins the World Cup."

For sports, the office, and for school, some parts of conversation are essential. What happens when you need to get to work but don't have any clean clothes to wear because of malfunctions with the machinery. What you need is to be able to pick up the phone and ask a professional or a friend, "My washing machine and dryer are broken so maybe I can wash my laundry at the public laundromat." When you finally head out after work for some drinks and meet a nice new man, you can say, "You can leave me a voicemail or send me a text message."

Hopefully, these examples help show you how reading all three parts of this series in combination will prepare you for all you need in order to boost your conversational learning skills and engage with others in your newly learned language. The first two books have been an important start. This third book adds additional vocabulary and will provide the comprehensive knowledge required.

OFFICE - BIROU

Boss – Patron (şef birou)
Employee(s) - Angajat(ţi)
Staff - Personal
Meeting - Întâlnire
Conference room - Sala de conferinţe
Secretary - Secretar/ **Receptionist -** Recepţioner
Schedule - Program
Calendar - Calendar
Supplies - Rechizite
Pencil - Creion/ **Pen -** Pix/ **Ink -** Cerneală/ **Eraser -** Radieră
Desk - Birou/ **Cubicle -** Cabină/ **Chair -** Scaun
Office furniture - Mobilier de birou
Business card - Carte de vizită
Lunch break - Pauză de masă
Days off - Zile libere
Briefcase - Servietă
Bathroom - Baie

My boss asked me to hand in the paperwork.
Şeful mi-a cerut să predau actele.
Our secretary isn't here today. The receptionist is here but she is in the bathroom.
Secretara noastră nu este aici astăzi. Recepţionera este aici, dar se află în baie.
The employee meeting can take place in the conference room.
Întâlnirea angajaţilor poate avea loc în sala de conferinţe.
My business cards are inside my briefcase.
Cărţile mele de vizită sunt în servietă.
The office staff must check their work schedule daily.
Personalul biroului trebuie să îşi verifice programul de lucru zilnic.
I am going to buy office furniture.
Voi achiziţiona mobilier de birou.
There isn't any ink in this pen.
Nu există cerneală în acest stilou.
This pencil is missing an eraser.
Acestui creion îi lipseşte o gumă de şters.
Our days off are written on the calendar.
Zilele noastre libere sunt înscrise în calendar.
I need to buy extra office supplies.
Trebuie să cumpăr rechizite suplimentare pentru birou.
I am busy until my lunch break.
Sunt ocupat până la pauza de masă.

Laptop - Laptop
Computer - Computer
Keyboard - Tastatură
Mouse - Maus
Email - E-Mail
Password - Parolă
Attachment - Ataşament
Printer - Imprimantă
Colored printer - Imprimantă color
To download - A descărca
To upload - A încărca
Internet - Internet
Account - Cont
A copy - O copie / **To copy -** A copia
Paste – Lipeşte (după copiere)
Fax - Fax
Scanner - Scanner **/ To scan -** A scana
Telephone - Telefon
Charger - Încărcător**/ To charge** (a phone) **-** A încărca (un telefon)

I want to write an important email but I forgot my password for my account.
Vreau să scriu un e-mail important, dar mi-am uitat parola contului meu.
I need to purchase a computer, a keyboard, a printer, and a desk.
Trebuie să cumpăr un computer, o tastatură, o imprimantă şi un birou.
Where is the mouse on my laptop?
Unde este mouse-ul pe laptopul meu?
The internet is slow today therefore it's difficult to upload or download.
Internetul este lent astăzi, de aceea este dificil de încărcat sau descărcat.
Do you have a colored printer?
Ai o imprimantă color?
I needed to fax the contract but instead, I decided to send it as an attachment in the email.
Trebuia să trimit contractul prin fax, dar, în schimb, am decis să-l trimit ca ataşament la e-mail.
One day, the fax machine will be completely obsolete.
Într-o zi, faxul va fi complet depăşit.
Where is my phone charger?
Unde este încărcătorul meu de telefon?
The scanner is broken.
Scanerul este stricat.
The telephone is behind the chair.
Telefonul este în spatele scaunului.

Shredder – Tocător (de hârtie)
Copy machine - Maşină de copiat
Filing cabinet - Dulap de dosare
Paper - Hârtie, **(p)** hârtii**/ Page -** Pagină, **(p)** pagini
Paperwork - Hârtii
Portfolio - Portofoliu
Files - Fişiere
Document - Document
Contract - Contract
Records – Înregistrări (dosare)/ **Archives -** Arhive
Deadline - Termen limită
Binder - Biblioraft
Paper clip - Agrafă
Stapler - Capsator**/ Staples -** Capse
Stamp - Ştampilă
Mail - Poştă
Letter - Scrisoare
Envelope - Plic
Data - Date / **Analysis -** Analiză
Highlighter - Evidenţiator/ **To highlight -** A evidenţia
Marker - Marcator
Ruler - Riglă

The supervisor at our company is responsible for data analysis.
Supraveghetorul companiei noastre este responsabil pentru analiza datelor.
The copy machine is next to the telephone.
Copiatorul este lângă telefon.
I can't find my stapler, paper clips, nor my highlighter in my cubicle.
Nu îmi găsesc capsatorul, agrafele de hârtie şi nici lanterna în dulap.
The filing cabinet is full of documents.
Fişetul este plin de documente.
The garbage can is full.
Coşul de gunoi este plin.
Give me the file because today is the deadline.
Dă-mi dosarul pentru că astăzi este termenul limită.
Where do I put the binder?
Unde pun biblioraftul?
The ruler is next to the shredder.
Rigla este lângă tocător.
I need a stamp and an envelope.
Am nevoie de o ştampilă şi un plic.
There is a letter in the mail.
Este o scrisoare în poştă.

SCHOOL - ŞCOALĂ

Student - Elev
Teacher - Profesor
Substitute teacher - Profesor suplinitor
A class - O clasă
A classroom - O sală de clasă
Education - Educaţie
Private school - Şcoală privată
Public school - Şcoală publică
Elementary school – Şcoală primară
Middle school - Şcoală gimnazială
High school - Liceu
University - Universitate/ **College** - Facultate
Grade (level) - Clasa/ **Grade** (grade on a test) – Notă (la un test)
Pass - Admis / **Fail** - Respins
Absent - Absent / **Present** - Prezent

The classroom is empty.
Sala de clasă este goală.
I want to bring my laptop to class.
Vreau să-mi aduc laptopul la clasă.
Our math teacher is absent and therefore a substitute teacher replaced him.
Profesorul nostru de matematică este absent şi, prin urmare, un profesor suplinitor l-a înlocuit.
All the students are present.
Toţi elevii sunt prezenţi.
Make sure to pass your classes because you can't fail this semester.
Asigură-te că îţi treci cursurile, pentru că nu poţi pica în acest semestru.
The education level at a private school is much more intense.
Nivelul de educaţie la o şcoală privată este mult mai intens.
I went to a public elementary and middle school.
Am fost la o şcoală primară şi gimnazială publică.
I have good memories of high school.
Am amintiri bune despre liceu.
My son is 15 years old and he is in the ninth grade.
Fiul meu are 15 ani şi este în clasa a IX-a.
You must get good grades on your report card.
Trebuie să obţii note bune în carnetul de note.
College textbooks are expensive.
Manualele de facultate sunt scumpe.
I want to study at an out-of-state university.
Vreau să studiez la o universitate din afara statului.

Subject - Subiect
Science - Știință/ **Chemistry** - Chimie/ **Physics** - Fizică
Geography - Geografie
History - Istorie
Math - Matematică
Addition - Adunare / **Subtraction** - Scădere
Division - Împărțire
Multiplication - Înmulțire
Language - Limbă/ **English** - Engleză/ **Foreign language** - Limbă străină
Physical education - Educație fizică
Chalk - Cretă/ **Board** - Tablă
Report card – Carnet de note
Alphabet - Alfabet/ **Letters** - Litere/ **Words** - Cuvinte
To review – A examina
Dictionary - Dicţionar
Detention - Detenție
The principle - Principiul

At school, geography is my favorite class, English is easy, math is hard, and history is boring.
La școală, geografia este ora mea preferată, engleza este ușoară, matematica este grea, iar istoria este plictisitoare.
After English class, there is physical education.
După ora de engleză, urmează educație fizică.
Today's math lesson is on addition and subtraction. Next month it will be division and multiplication.
Lecția de matematică de astăzi este cu adunări și scăderi. Luna viitoare va fi împărțirea și înmulțirea.
This year for foreign language credits, I want to choose Spanish and French.
Anul acesta, pentru credite pe limbi străine, vreau să aleg spaniola și franceza.
I want to buy a dictionary, thesaurus, and a journal for school.
Vreau să cumpăr un dicționar, tezaur și un jurnal pentru școală.
The teacher needs to write the homework on the board with chalk.
Profesorul trebuie să scrie temele pe tablă cu cretă.
Today the students have to review the letters of the alphabet.
Astăzi elevii trebuie să recapituleze literele alfabetului.
The teacher wants to teach the students roman numerals.
Profesorul dorește să învețe elevii cifrele romane.
If you can't behave well then you must go to the principal's office, and maybe stay after school for detention.
Dacă nu poți să te comporți frumos, atunci trebuie să mergi în biroul directorului și poate să rămâi după ore pentru detenție.

Test - Test/ **Quiz** - Test surpriză
Lesson - Lecție/ **Notes** - Note
Homework - Temă pentru acasă / **Assignment** - Sarcină/ **Project** - Proiect
Pencil - Creion/ **Pen** - Pix/ **Ink** - Cerneală/ **Eraser** - Radieră
Backpack – Ghiozdan
Book - Carte/ **Folders** - Fişiere/ **Notebook** - Caiet / **Papers** - Hârtii
Calculator - Calculator
Glue - Lipici/ **Scissors** - Foarfece / **Adhesive tape** - Bandă adezivă
Lunchbox - Pachet de prânz / **Lunch** - Prânz/ **Cafeteria** - Cantină
Kindergarten - Grădiniță/ **Pre-school** - Preşcolar/ **Day care** - Centrul de zi
Triangle - Triunghi/ **Square** - Pătrat/ **Circle** - Cerc
Crayons - Creioane colorate

Today, we don't have a test but we have a surprise quiz.
Astăzi, nu avem un test, dar avem o lucrare surpriză.
Are a pen, a pencil, and an eraser included with the school supplies?
Sunt incluse un pix, un creion şi o radieră în rechizitele şcolare?
I think my notebook and calculator are in my backpack.
Caietul şi calculatorul cred că sunt în rucsac.
All my papers are in my folder.
Toate actele mele sunt în dosarul meu.
I need glue and scissors for my project.
Am nevoie de lipici şi foarfece pentru proiectul meu.
I need tape and a stapler to fix my book.
Am nevoie de bandă adezivă şi un capsator pentru a-mi repara cartea.
You have to concentrate in order to take notes.
Trebuie să te concentrezi pentru a lua notițe.
The school librarian wants to invite the art and music teacher to the library next week.
Bibliotecarul şcolii vrea să-l invite pe profesorul de artă şi muzică la bibliotecă săptămâna viitoare.
For lunch, your children can purchase food at the cafeteria or they can bring food from home.
La prânz, copiii dumneavoastră pot cumpăra mâncare de la cantină sau pot aduce mâncare de acasă.
I forgot my lunchbox and crayons at home.
Mi-am uitat acasă pachețelul de prânz şi creioanele colorate.
To draw shapes such as a triangle, square, circle, and rectangle is easy.
Este uşor să desenezi forme precum triunghi, pătrat, cerc şi dreptunghi.
During the week, my youngest child is at daycare, my middle one is in pre-school, and the oldest is in kindergarten.
În timpul săptămânii, cel mai mic copil al meu este la creşă, cel mijlociu este la şcoală, iar cel mare la grădiniță.

PROFESSION - PROFESIE

Doctor - Medic / **Nurse** - Asistentă /**Veterinarian** - Medic veterinar
Psychologist - Psiholog/ **Psychiatrist** - Psihiatru
Lawyer - Avocat/ **Judge** - Judecător
Pilot - Pilot / **Flight attendant** - Însoțitor de zbor
Reporter - Reporter / **Journalist** - Jurnalist
Electrician - Electrician / **Mechanic** - Mecanic
Investigator - Anchetator / **Detective** - Detectiv
Translator - Traducător
Producer - Producător/ **Director** - Regizor

What's your profession?
Care este profesia ta?
I am going to medical school to study medicine because I want to be a doctor.
Mă duc la facultatea de medicină pentru a studia medicina fiindcă vreau să fiu doctor.
There is a difference between a psychologist and a psychiatrist.
Există o diferență între un psiholog și un psihiatru.
Most children want to be an astronaut, a veterinarian, or an athlete.
Majoritatea copiilor vor să fie astronaut, medic veterinar sau atlet.
The judge spoke to the lawyer at the court house.
Judecătorul i-a vorbit avocatului la tribunal.
The police investigator needs to investigate this case.
Anchetatorul de poliție trebuie să investigheze acest caz.
Being a detective could be a fun job.
A fi detectiv ar putea fi o muncă distractivă.
The flight attendant and the pilot are on the plane.
Însoțitorul de bord și pilotul sunt în avion.
I am a certified electrician.
Sunt electrician autorizat.
The mechanic overcharged me.
Mecanicul m-a suprataxat.
I want to be a journalist.
Vreau să fiu jurnalist.
The best translators work at my company.
Cei mai buni traducători lucrează la compania mea.
Are you a photographer?
Esti fotograf?
The author wants to hire a ghostwriter to write his book.
Autorul vrea să angajeze un scriitor-fantomă pentru a-și scrie cartea.
I want to find the directors of the company.
Vreau să găsesc administratorii societății.

Artist (performer) **-** Artist (interpret)
Artist (draws paints picture) **-** Artist (desenează și pictează)
Author - Autor
Painter - Pictor
Dancer - Dansator
Writer - Scriitor
Photographer - Fotograf
A cook - Un bucătar **/ A chef -** Un chef bucătar
Waiter - Chelner **/ Bartender -** Barman
Barber shop - Frizerie**/ Barber -** Frizer / **Stylist -** Stilist
Maid - Servitoare/ **Housekeeper -** Menajeră
Caretaker - Îngrijitor
Farmer - Fermier**/ Gardner -** Grădinar
Mailman - Poștaș
A guard - Un gardian
A cashier - Un casier

The artist produced this artwork for her catalog.
Artista a produs această opera de artă pentru catalogul ei.
The artist drew a sketch.
Artistul a desenat o schiță.
I want to apply as a cook at the restaurant instead of as a waiter.
Vreau să aplic pe poziția de bucătar la restaurant și nu ca ospătar.
The gardener can only come on weekdays.
Grădinarul poate veni doar în zilele lucrătoare.
I have to go to the barbershop now.
Trebuie să merg la frizerie acum.
Being a bartender isn't an easy job.
A fi barman nu este o meserie ușoară.
Why do we need another maid?
De ce avem nevoie de o altă menajeră?
I want to file a complaint against the mailman.
Vreau să depun o plângere împotriva poștașului.
I am a part-time artist.
Sunt un artist cu jumătate de normă.
She was a dancer at the play.
A fost dansatoare la piesă.
You need to contact the insurance company if you want to find another caretaker.
Trebuie să contactați compania de asigurări dacă doriți să găsiți un alt îngrijitor.
The farmer can sell us ripened tomatoes today.
Fermierul ne poate vinde astăzi roșii coapte.

BUSINESS - AFACERE

A business - O afacere/ **Company** - Societate/ **Factory** - Fabrică
A professional - Un profesionist / **Secretary** - Secretar
Position - Post/ **Work, job** - Muncă/ **Employee** - Angajat
Owner - Proprietar/ **Manager** - Manager/ **Management** - Administrație
An interview - Un interviu/ **Resumé** – Curriculum vitae
Presentation - Prezentare / **Specialist** - Specialist
To hire - De angajat/ **To fire** - A demite
Pay check - Cec de plată / **Income** - Venituri/ **Salary** - Salariu
Insurance - Asigurare/ **Benefits** - Beneficii
Trimester - Trimestru/ **Budget** - Buget / **Net** - Net / **Gross** - Brut
To retire - A se pensiona/ **Pension** - Pensiune

I need a job.
Am nevoie de un loc de muncă.
She is the secretary of the company.
Ea este secretara societății.
The manager needs to hire another employee.
Managerul trebuie să angajeze un alt angajat.
I am lucky because I have an interview for a cashier position today.
Sunt norocos pentru că am un interviu pentru un post de casier astăzi.
How much is the salary and does it include benefits?
Cât este salariul și include beneficii?
Management has your resumé and they need to show it to the owner of the company.
Conducerea are CV-ul dvs. și trebuie să-l arate proprietarului companiei.
I am at work at the factory now.
Sunt la serviciu acum la fabrică.
In business, you should be professional.
În afaceri, ar trebui să fii profesionist.
Is the presentation ready?
Este gata prezentarea?
The first trimester is part of the annual budget.
Primul trimestru face parte din bugetul anual.
I have to see the net and gross profits of the business.
Trebuie să văd profitul net și brut al afacerii.
I want to retire already.
Vreau să mă pensionez deja.
My position in the company is marketing and I am responsible for advertising and ads.
Postul meu în sociteate este în marketing și sunt responsabil pentru publicitate și reclame.

Client - Client / **A purchase** - O achiziție
Broker - Intermediar / **Salesperson -** Agent de vânzări
Realtor - Agent imobiliar **/ Real Estate Market -** Piața imobiliară
A lease - Un contract de închiriere / **To lease -** De închiriat
To invest - A investi **/ Investment -** Investiție
Landlord - Proprietar**/ Tenant -** Chiriaș
Economy - Economie**/ Mortgage -** Ipotecă
Interest rate - Rata dobânzii **/ A loan -** Un împrumut
Commission - Comisie**/ Percent -** Procent
A sale - O vânzare **/ Value -** Valoare**/ Profit -** Profit
The demand - Cererea**/ The supply -** Oferta
A contract - Un contract **/ Terms -** Condiții
Signature - Semnătură**/ Initials -** Inițiale
Stock - Acțiuni**/ Stock broker -** Agent de bursă
Advertisement - Publicitate **/ Ads -** Reclame
To advertise - A face publicitate

I can earn a huge profit from stocks.
Pot câștiga un profit uriaș din acțiuni.
The demand in the real estate market depends on the country's economy.
Cererea pe piața imobiliară depinde de economia țării.
If you want to sell your home, I can recommend a very good realtor.
Dacă doriți să vă vindeți casa, vă pot recomanda un agent imobiliar foarte bun.
The investor wants to invest in this shopping center because of its good potential.
Investitorul dorește să investească în acest centru comercial datorită potențialului său bun.
The value of the property increased by twenty percent.
Valoarea proprietății a crescut cu douăzeci la sută.
How much is the commission on the sale?
Cât este comisionul la vânzare?
The client wants to lease instead of purchasing the property.
Clientul dorește să închirieze în loc să cumpere proprietatea.
What are the terms of the purchase?
Care sunt condițiile de achiziție?
I can negotiate a better interest rate.
Pot negocia o dobândă mai bună.
I need a small loan in order to pay my mortgage this month.
Am nevoie de un mic împrumut pentru a-mi plăti ipoteca luna aceasta.
I need a signature and initials on the contract.
Am nevoie de semnătură și inițiale pe contract.

Money - Bani/ **Currency –** Monedă
Cash - Numerar/ **Coins -** Monede
Change (change for a bill) – Rest (mărunțiș la o factură)
Credit - Credit
Tax - Taxă
Price - Preț
Invoice - Factură
Inventory - Stoc / **Merchandise -** Marfă
A refund - O restituire
Product - Produs / **Produced -** Produs
Retail - Comerț cu amănuntul
Wholesale - Comerț cu ridicata
Imports - Importuri/ **Exports -** Exporturi
To ship - A expedia
Shipment - Livrare

Don't forget to bring cash with you.
Nu uita să ai bani la tine.
Do you have change for a 100 Euro bill?
Aveți schimb pentru o bancnotă de 100 de euro?
I don't have a credit card.
Nu am un card de credit.
The salesperson told me there is no refund.
Agentul de vânzări mi-a spus că nu există nicio restituție.
This product is produced in Italy.
Acest produs este produs in Italia.
I work in the export/import business.
Lucrez în domeniul exportului/importului.
Let me check my inventory.
Lasă-mă să-mi verific inventarul.
This product is insured.
Acest produs este asigurat.
This invoice contains a mistake.
Această factură conține o greșeală.
What is the wholesale and retail value of this shipment?
Care este valoarea angro și cu amănuntul a acestei expedieri?
You don't have enough money to purchase the merchandise.
Nu ai suficienți bani pentru a cumpăra marfa.
How much does the shipping cost and is it in foreign currency?
Cât costă transportul și dacă este în valută?
There is a tax exemption on this income.
Există o scutire de impozit pentru acest venit.

SPORTS - SPORT

Basketball - Baschet/ **Soccer** - Fotbal
Game - Joc/ **Stadium** - Stadion / **Ball** - Minge/ **Player** - Jucător
To jump - A sări / **To throw** - A arunca
To kick - A da cu piciorul /**To catch** - A prinde
Coach - Antrenor/ **Referee** - Arbitru
Competition - Competiție
Team - Echipă/ **Teammate** - Coechipier
National team - Echipă națională
Opponent - Adversar
Half time - La jumătatea timpului / **Finals** - Finală
The goal - Golul/ **A goal** - Un gol / **Scores** - Scoruri
To lose - A pierde / **A Defeat** - O înfrângere
To win - A câștiga / **A victory** - O victorie
The looser – Pierzătorul / **The winner** - Câștigătorul
Field - Câmp / **Helmet** - Cască / **Basket** - Coș
Fans - Fani
Penalty - Penalty

I like to watch basketball games.
Îmi place să mă uit la meciuri de baschet.
Soccer is my favorite sport.
Fotbalul este sportul meu preferat.
To play basketball, you need to be good at throwing and jumping.
Pentru a juca baschet, trebuie să fii bun la aruncat și sărituri.
The national team has a lot of fans.
Echipa națională are mulți suporteri.
My teammate can't find his helmet.
Coechipierul meu nu își găsește casca.
The coach and the team were on the field during half-time.
Antrenorul și echipa au fost pe teren la pauză.
The coach needs to bring his team today to meet the new referee.
Antrenorul trebuie să-și aducă astăzi echipa pentru a-l întâlni pe noul arbitru.
Our opponents went home after their defeat.
Adversarii noștri au plecat acasă după înfrângere.
I have tickets to a soccer game at the stadium.
Am bilete la un meci de fotbal pe stadion.
The player received a penalty for kicking the ball in the wrong goal.
Jucătorul a primit penalty pentru că a lovit mingea în poarta greșită.
Not every person likes sports.
Nu tuturor le place sportul.

Athlete - Atlet/ **Olympics -** Olimpiadă/ **World cup -** Cupă Mondială
Bicycle - Bicicletă/ **Cyclist -** Ciclist/ **Swimming -** Înot
Wrestling - Lupte/ **Boxing -** Box/ **Martial arts -** Arte marțiale
Championship - Campionat/ **Award -** Premiu/ **Tournament -** Turneu
Horse racing - Curse de cai / **Racing -** Curse
Exercise - Exercițiu/ **Fitness -** Fitness / **Gym -** Sală de sport
Captain - Căpitan/ **Judge -** Judecător / **Trainer -** Formator
A match - Un meci / **Rules -** Reguli/ **Track -** Pistă
Pool (billiards) **-** Biliard
Pool (swimming pool) **–** Piscină (piscină)

Today are the finals for the Olympic Games.
Astăzi sunt finalele Jocurilor Olimpice.
Let's see who wins the World Cup.
Să vedem cine câștigă Cupa Mondială.
I want to compete in the cycling championship.
Vreau să concurez în campionatul de ciclism.
I am an athlete so I must stay in shape.
Sunt un atlet, așa că trebuie să rămân în formă.
After my boxing lesson, I want to go and swim in the pool.
După lecția mea de box, vreau să merg să înot în piscină.
He will receive an award because he is the winner of the martial-arts tournament.
El va primi un premiu pentru că este câștigătorul turneului de arte marțiale.
The wrestling captain must teach his team the rules of the game.
Căpitanul de lupte trebuie să-și învețe echipa regulile jocului.
At the horse-racing competition, the judge couldn't announce the score.
La concursul de curse de cai, arbitrul nu a putut anunța scorul.
There is a bicycle race at the park today.
Astăzi este o cursă de biciclete în parc.
This fitness program is expensive.
Acest program de fitness este scump.
It's healthy to go to the gym every day.
Este sănătos să mergi la sală în fiecare zi.
Weightlifting is good exercise.
Ridicarea greutăților este un exercițiu bun.
I want to run on the track today.
Vreau să alerg pe pistă azi.
I like to win in billiards.
Îmi place să câștig la biliard.
Skateboarding is forbidden here.
Skateboarding-ul este interzis aici.

OUTDOOR ACTIVITIES - ACTIVITĂȚI ÎN EXTERIOR

Hiking - Drumeții
Hiking trail - Traseu de drumeții
Pocket knife - Cuțit de buzunar
Compass - Busolă
Camping - Loc de camping / **A camp** – Un loc de camping
Campground - Camping / **Tent** - Cort / **RV** - rulotă
Campfire - Foc de tabără / **Matches** - Meciuri/ **Lighter** - Brichetă
Flame - Flacără / **The smoke** - Fumul / **Coal** - Cărbune
Fishing - Pescuit/ **To fish** - A pescui
Fishing pole - Undiță/ **Fishing line** - Fir de pescuit
Hook - Cârlig/ **A float** – O plută / **A weight** - O greutate/ **Bait** - Momeală
Fishing net - Plasa de pescuit
To hunt - A vâna / **Rifle** - Pușcă

I enjoy hiking on the trail, with my compass and my pocketknife.
Îmi place să fac drumeții pe trasee, cu busola și cu briceagul meu de buzunar.
Don't forget the water bottle in your backpack.
Nu uita de sticla de apă din rucsac.
There aren't any tents at the campground.
Nu sunt corturi în zona de camping.
I want to sleep in an RV instead of a tent.
Vreau să dorm într-o rulotă în loc de cort.
We can use a lighter to start a campfire.
Putem folosi o brichetă pentru a aprinde un foc de tabără.
We need coal and matches for the trip.
Avem nevoie de cărbune și chibrituri pentru călătorie.
Put out the fire because the flames are very high and there is a lot of smoke.
Stingeți focul pentru că flăcările sunt foarte mari și este mult fum.
There is fog outside and the temperature is below freezing.
Afară este ceață și temperatura este sub limita de îngheț.
Where is the fishing store? I need to buy hooks, fishing line, bait, and a net.
Unde este magazinul de pescuit? Trebuie să cumpăr cârlige, gută, momeală și o plasă.
You can't bring your fishing pole or your hunting rifle to the campground of the State Park because there is a sign there which says, "No fishing and no hunting."
Nu vă puteți aduce undița de pescuit sau pușca de vânătoare în zona de camping a parcului de stat, pentru că acolo există un semn pe care scrie: "Pescuit și vânătoare interzise".

Sailing - Navigație
A sail - O velă
Sailboat - Barcă cu pânze
Rowing - Canotaj
A paddle - O vâslă
Motor - Motor
Canoe - Canoe / **Kayak -** Caiac
Rock climbing - Alpinism
Horseback riding - Călărie
Diver - Scafandru / **Scuba diving -** Scufundări
Skydiving - Parașutism
Parachute - Parașută / **Paragliding -** Parapantă
Hot air balloon - Balon cu aer cald
Kite - Zmeu
Surfing - Surfing / **Surf board -** Placă de surf
Ice skating - Patinaj pe gheață / **Skiing -** Schi

With a broken motor, we need a paddle to row the boat.
Cu motorul stricat, avem nevoie de o vâslă pentru a vâsli barca.
It's important to know how to use a sail before sailing on a sailboat.
Este important să știți cum să folosiți o velă înainte de a naviga cu o barcă cu pânze.
In my opinion, a kayak is much more fun than a canoe.
După părerea mea, un caiac este mult mai distractiv decât o canoe.
Do I need to bring my scuba certification in order to scuba dive at the coral reef?
Trebuie să-mi aduc brevetul de scafandru pentru a face scufundări la reciful de corali?
I have my mask, snorkel, and fins.
Am masca, tubul de respirație și aripioarele.
I don't know which is scarier, sky diving or paragliding.
Nu știu ce este mai înfricoșător, săritura cu parașuta sau parapanta.
There are several outdoor activities here including rock climbing and horseback riding.
Există mai multe activități în aer liber aici, inclusiv alpinism și călărie.
My dream was always to fly in a hot-air balloon.
Visul meu a fost mereu să zbor într-un balon cu aer cald.
We are going skiing on our next vacation.
Mergem la schi în următoarea vacanță.
Where is the surfboard? I want to surf the waves at the beach.
Unde este placa de surf? Vreau să fac surf pe valurile de pe plajă.
Ice skating is much easier than it seems.
Patinajul este mult mai ușor decât pare.

ELECTRICAL DEVICES - DISPOZITIVE ELECTRICE

Electronic - Electronic/ **Electricity -** Electricitate
Appliance - Electrocasnic
Oven - Cuptor **/ Stove -** Aragaz
Microwave - Cuptor cu microunde
Refrigerator - Frigider/ **Freezer -** Congelator
Coffee maker - Filtru de cafea/ **Coffee pot-** Oală de cafea
Toaster - Toaster
Dishwasher - Mașină de spălat vase
Laundry machine - Mașină de spălat rufe/**Dryer -** Uscător
Laundry - Spălătorie
Fan - Ventilator/ **Air condition -** Aer condiționat
Alarm - Alarmă
Smoke detector - Detector de fum
Battery - Baterie

He needs to pay his electric bill if he wants electricity.
Trebuie să-și plătească factura la electricitate dacă vrea electricitate.
I want to purchase a few things at the electronic appliance store.
Vreau să cumpăr câteva lucruri de la magazinul de electrocasnice.
I can't put plastic utensils in the dishwasher.
Nu pot pune ustensile de plastic în mașina de spălat vase.
I am going to get rid of my microwave and oven because they are not functioning.
Am de gând să scap de cuptorul cu microunde și cuptorul meu pentru că nu funcționează.
The refrigerator and freezer aren't cold enough.
Frigiderul și congelatorul nu sunt suficient de reci.
The coffee maker and toaster are in the kitchen.
Filtrul de cafea și prăjitorul de pâine sunt în bucătărie.
My washing machine and dryer do not function therefore I must wash my laundry at the public laundromat.
Mașina de spălat și uscătorul meu nu funcționează, așa că trebuie să îmi spăl rufele la spălătoria publică.
Is this fan new?
Acest ventilator este nou?
Unfortunately, the new air conditioner unit hasn't been delivered yet.
Din păcate, noua unitate de aer condiționat nu a fost încă livrată.
Is that annoying sound the alarm clock or the fire alarm?
Acel sunet enervant este ceasul deșteptător sau alarma de incendiu?
The smoke detector needs new batteries.
Detectorul de fum are nevoie de baterii noi.

Lamp - Lampă / **Stereo** - Stereo
A (wall) clock - Un ceas (de perete) / **A watch** - Un ceas de mână
Vacuum cleaner - Aspirator
Phone - Telefon/ **Text message** - Mesaj text
Voice message - Mesaj vocal
Camera – Cameră
Flashlight - Lanternă/ **Light** - Lumină
Furnace - Cuptor/ **Heater** - Aerotermă
Cord - Şnur/ **Charger** - Încărcător / **Outlet** - Priză
Headsets - Căşti
Doorbell - Sonerie
Lawn mower - Maşină de tuns iarba

The clock is hanging on the wall.
Ceasul este atârnat de perete.
The cordless stereo is on the table.
Aparatul de radio fără fir este pe masă.
I still have a home telephone.
Încă mai am un telefon fix acasă.
I need to buy a lamp and a vacuum cleaner today.
Trebuie să cumpăr o lampă şi un aspirator astăzi.
In the past, cameras were more common. Today, everyone can use their phones to take pictures.
În trecut, aparatele de fotografiat erau mai frecvente. Astăzi, toată lumea îşi poate folosi telefoanele pentru a face fotografii.
You can leave me a voice message or send me a text message.
Puteţi să-mi lăsaţi un mesaj vocal sau să-mi trimiteţi un mesaj text.
The lights don't function when there is a blackout therefore I must rely on my flashlight.
Luminile nu funcţionează atunci când există o întrerupere, aşa că trebuie să mă bazez pe lanterna mea.
I can't hear the doorbell.
Nu aud soneria.
There is a higher risk of causing a house fire from an electric heater than a furnace.
Există un risc mai mare de a provoca un incendiu în casă de la un încălzitor electric decât de la un cuptor.
I need to connect the cord to the outlet.
Trebuie să conectez cablul la priză.
His lawnmower is very noisy.
Maşina lui de tuns iarba este foarte zgomotoasă.
Why is my headset on the floor?
De ce se află căştile mele pe podea?

TOOLS - INSTRUMENTE

Toolbox - Cutie de instrumente
Carpenter - Tâmplar
Hammer - Ciocan
Saw - Fierăstrău/ **Axe** - Topor
A drill - Un burghiu / **To drill** - A găuri
Nail - Cui/ **A screw** - Un şurub
Screwdriver - Şurubelniţă/ **A wrench** - O cheie/ **Pliers** - Cleşti
Paint brush - Pensulă/ **To paint** - A picta/ **The paint** - Vopsea
Ladder - Scară
Rope - Funie/ **String** - Coardă
A scale - O scară/ **Measuring tape** - Bandă de măsurare
Machine - Utilaj
A lock - Un lacăt / **Locked** - Încuiat/ **To lock** - A încuia
Equipment - Echipament
Metal - Metal/ **Steel** - Oţel/ **Iron** - Fier
Broom - Mătură/ **Dust pan** - Tavă de praf
Bucket - Găleată/ **Sponge** - Burete / **Mop** - Mop
Shovel - Lopată/ **A trowel** - O mistrie

The carpenter needs nails, a hammer, a saw, and a drill.
Tâmplarul are nevoie de cuie, un ciocan, un ferăstrău și un burghiu.
The string is very long. Where are the scissors?
Sfoara este foarte lungă. Unde sunt foarfecele?
The screwdriver is in the toolbox.
Șurubelnița este în cutia de instrumente.
This tool can cut through metal.
Acest instrument poate tăia metalul.
The ladder is next to the tools.
Scara este lângă unelte.
I must buy a brush to paint the walls.
Trebuie să cumpăr o pensulă pentru a picta pereții.
The paint bucket is empty.
Găleata de vopsea este goală.
It's better to tie the shovel with a rope in my pick-up truck.
Este mai bine să-mi leg lopata cu o frânghie în camionetă.
How can I fix this machine?
Cum pot repara acest utilaj?
The broom and dust pan are with the rest of my cleaning equipment.
Matura și tava de praf sunt cu restul echipamentului meu de curățare.
Where did you put the mop and the bucket?
Unde ai pus mopul și găleata?

CAR - AUTOMOBIL

Engine - Motor
Ignition - Aprindere
Steering wheel - Volan
Automatic - Automatic
Manual - Manual
Gear shift - Schimbător de viteze
Seat - Scaun
Seat belt - Centura de siguranță
Airbag - Airbag
Brakes - Frâne
Handbrake - Frână de mână
Baby seat - Scaun pentru copii
Driver seat - Scaun şofer
Passenger seat - Scaun pasager
Front seat - Scaun din față
Back seat - Scaun din spate
Car passenger - Pasager în autoturism
Warning light - Lampă de avertizare
Button - Buton/ **Horn** (of the car) – Claxon (al maşinii)

When driving, both hands must be on the steering wheel.
Când conduceți, ambele mâini trebuie să fie pe volan.
I must take my car to my mechanic because there is a problem with the ignition.
Trebuie să-mi duc maşina la mecanic pentru că este o problemă cu aprinderea.
What happened to the engine?
Ce s-a întâmplat cu motorul?
The seat is missing a seat belt.
Scaunului îi lipseste o centură de siguranță.
I prefer a gear shift instead of an automatic car.
Prefer un schimbător de viteze manual în locul unei maşini automate.
The brakes are new in this vehicle
Frânele sunt noi la acest vehicul
This vehicle doesn't have a handbrake.
Acest vehicul nu are frână de mână.
There is an airbag on both the driver side and the passenger side.
Există un airbag atât pe partea şoferului, cât și pe partea pasagerului.
The baby seat is in the back seat.
Scaunul pentru copii este pe bancheta din spate.
The warning light button is located next to the steering wheel.
Butonul luminos de avertizare este situat lângă volan.

Windshield - Parbriz
Windshield wiper - Ștergător de parbriz
Windshield fluid - Lichid de parbriz
Rear view mirror - Oglinda retrovizoare
Side mirror - Oglindă laterală
Door handle - Mânerul ușii
Spare tire - Anvelopă de rezervă
Trunk - Portbagajul
Hood (of the vehicle) **–** Capotă (a unui vehicul)
Alarm - Alarmă
Window - Fereastra
Drive license - Permis de conducere
License plate - Plăcuță de înmatriculare
Gasoline - Benzină
Low fuel - Nivel redus de combustibil
Flat tire - Anvelopă desumflată
Crowbar - Rangă
A (car) jack - Un cric
Wrench - Cheie

The windshield and all four of my car windows are cracked.
Parbrizul și toate cele patru geamuri ale mașinii mele sunt crăpate.
I want to clean my rear-view mirror and my side mirrors.
Vreau să-mi curăț oglinda retrovizoare și oglinzile laterale.
My car doesn't have an alarm.
Mașina mea nu are alarmă.
Does this car have a spare tire in the trunk?
Această mașină are o roată de rezervă în portbagaj?
Please, close the car door.
Te rog, închide portiera.
Where is the nearest gas station?
Unde este cea mai apropiată stație de benzină?
The windshield wipers are new.
Ștergătoarele de parbriz sunt noi.
The door handle on the driver's side doesn't function.
Mânerul ușii de pe partea șoferului nu funcționează.
Your license plate has expired.
Numărul dvs. de înmatriculare a expirat.
I want to renew my driving license today.
Vreau să îmi reînnoiesc permisul de conducere astăzi.
Are the car doors locked?
Sunt portierele încuiate?

NATURE - NATURĂ

A plant - O plantă
Forest - Pădure
Tree - Arbore / **Trunk** - Trunchi
Branch - Creangă/ **Leaf** - Frunză/ **Root** - Rădăcină
Flower - Floare
Petal - Petală
Blossom - Floare
Stem - Tulpină/ **Seed** - Sământă
Rose - Trandafir
Nectar - Nectar/ **Pollen** - Polen
Vegetation - Vegetaţie/ **Bush** - Tufiş/ **Grass** - Iarbă
Rain forest - Pădure tropicală / **Tropical** - Tropical / **Palm tree** - Palmier
Season - Sezon/ **Spring** - Primavară/**Summer** - Vară/
Winter - Iarnă/**Autumn** - Toamnă

I want to collect a few leaves during the fall.
Vreau să adun câteva frunze în timpul toamnei.
There aren't any plants in the desert during this season.
Nu există plante în deşert în acest sezon.
The trees need rain.
Copacii au nevoie de ploaie.
The trunk, the branches, and the roots are all parts of the tree.
Trunchiul, ramurile şi rădăcinile sunt toate părţi ale copacului.
My rose bushes are beautiful.
Tufele mele de trandafiri sunt frumoase.
Where can I plant the seeds?
Unde pot planta seminţele?
I must trim the grass and vegetation in my garden.
Trebuie să-mi tund iarba şi vegetaţia din grădină.
The rain forest is a nature preserve.
Pădurea tropicală este o rezervaţie naturală.
Palm trees can only grow in a tropical climate.
Palmierii pot creşte doar într-un climat tropical.
I am allergic to pollen.
Sunt alergic la polen.
The orchid needs to bloom because I want to see its beautiful petals.
Orhideea trebuie să înflorească pentru că vreau să-i văd petalele frumoase.
Is the nectar from the flower sweet?
Nectarul din floare este dulce?
Be careful because the plant stem can break very easily.
Aveţi grijă pentru că tulpina plantei se poate rupe foarte uşor.

Lake - Lac
Sea - Mare
Ocean - Ocean
Waterfall - Cascadă
River - Râu**/ Canal -** Canal**/ Swamp -** Mlaştină
Mountain - Munte**/ Hill -** Deal
Rainbow - Curcubeu
Cloud - Nor
Lightning - Fulger**/ Thunder -** Tunet
Rain - Ploaie**/ Snow -** Zăpadă
Ice - Gheaţă**/ Hail -** Grindină
Fog - Ceaţă / **Dew -** Roua
Wind - Vânt**/ Air -** Aer
Sunset - Apus de soare**/ Sunrise -** Răsărit

There is a rainbow above the waterfall.
Este un curcubeu deasupra cascadei.
The ocean is bigger than the sea.
Oceanul este mai mare decât marea.
From the mountain, I can see the river.
De pe munte, văd râul.
Today we hope to see snow.
Astăzi sperăm să vedem zăpadă.
There aren't any clouds in the sky.
Nu este niciun nor pe cer.
I see the lightning from my window.
Văd fulgerul de la fereastra mea.
I can hear the thunder from outside.
Pot auzi tunetul de afară.
I want to see the sunset from the hill.
Vreau să văd apusul de pe deal.
The lake has a shallow part and a deep part.
Lacul are o parte puţin adâncă şi o parte adâncă.
I don't like the wind.
Nu-mi place vântul.
The air on the mountain is very clear.
Aerul de pe munte este foarte limpede.
Every dawn, there is dew on the leaves of my plants.
La fiecare răsărit, este rouă pe frunzele plantelor mele.
Is this ice or hail?
Aceasta este gheaţă sau grindină?
I can see the volcano.
Pot vedea vulcanul.

Sky - Cer
World - Lume/ **Earth -** Pământ
Sun - Soare/ **Moon -** Lună
Crescent - Semilună/ **Full moon -** Lună plină
Star - Stea/ **Planet -** Planetă
Fire - Foc/ **Heat -** Căldură/ **Humidity -** Umiditate
Agriculture - Agricultură
Island - Insulă / **Cave -** Peșteră
Public park - Parc public/ **National park -** Parc național
Rock - Stâncă/ **Stone -** Piatră
Ground - Pământ / **Soil -** Sol
Sea shore - Malul mării / **Seashell -** Scoică
Dawn - Zori / **Ray -** Rază
Dry - Uscat/ **Wet -** Umed
Deep - Adânc/ **Shallow –** Puțin adânc
Weeds - Buruieni
A stick - Un băţ
Dust - Praf

The moon and the stars are beautiful in the night sky.
Luna și stelele sunt frumoase pe cerul nopții.
The earth is a planet.
Pământul este o planetă.
The heat today is unbearable.
Căldura de astăzi este insuportabilă.
At the beach there is fresh air.
La plajă este aer curat.
I want to sail to the island to see the sunrise.
Vreau să navighez pe insulă pentru a vedea răsăritul.
Parts of the cave are dry and other parts are wet.
Părți ale peșterii sunt uscate, iar alte părți sunt umede.
We live in a beautiful world.
Trăim într-o lume frumoasă.
There is dust from the fire in the park.
Este praf de la focul din parc.
I want to collect seashells from the seashore.
Vreau să adun scoici de pe malul mării.
There are too many stones in the soil so it's impossible to use this area for agricultural purposes.
Sunt prea multe pietre în sol, așa că este imposibil să folosiți această zonă în scopuri agricole.
Why are there so many weeds growing by the swamp?
De ce cresc atâtea buruieni lângă mlaștină?

ANIMALS - Animale

Pet - Animal de companie
Mammals - Mamifere
Dog - Câine/ **Cat -** Pisică
Parrot - Papagal
Pigeon - Porumbel
Pig - Porc
Sheep - Oaie
Cow - Vacă/ **Bull -** Taur
Donkey - Măgar/ **Horse -** Cal
Camel - Cămilă
Rodent - Rozatoare
Mouse - Șoarece/ **Rat -** Șobolan
Rabbit - Iepure/ **Hamster -** Hamster
Duck - Rață/ **Goose -** Gâscă
Turkey - Curcan/ **Chicken -** Pui/ **Poultry -** Păsări de curte
Squirrel - Veveriță

I have a dog and two cats.
Am un câine și două pisici.
There is a bird on the tree.
Este o pasăre pe copac.
I want to go to the zoo to see the animals.
Vreau să merg la grădina zoologică să văd animalele.
My daughter wants a pet horse.
Fiica mea vrea un cal ca animal de companie.
A pig, a sheep, a donkey, and a cow are considered farm animals.
Un porc, o oaie, un măgar și o vacă sunt considerate animale de fermă.
I want a hamster as a pet.
Vreau un hamster ca animal de companie.
A camel is a desert animal.
O cămilă este un animal din deșert.
Can I put ducks, geese, and turkeys inside my coop?
Pot să-mi pun rațe, gâște și curcani în coteț?
We have rabbits and squirrels in our yard.
Avem iepuri și veverițe în curtea noastră.
It's cruel to keep a parrot inside a cage.
Este crud să ții un papagal într-o cușcă.
There are many pigeons in the city.
În oraș sunt mulți porumbei.
Mice and rats are rodents.
Șoarecii și șobolanii sunt rozătoare.

Lion - Leu
Hyena - Hienă
Leopard - Leopard / **Panther -** Panteră
Cheetah - Ghepard
Elephant - Elefant
Rhinoceros - Rinocer / **Hippopotamus -** Hipopotam
Bat - Liliac
Fox - Vulpe/ **Wolf -** Lup
Weasel - Nevăstuică
Bear - Urs
Tiger - Tigru
Deer - Cerb
Monkey - Maimuță
Otter - Vidră
Marsupial - Marsupial

There are a lot of animals in the forest.
Sunt multe animale în pădure.
The most dangerous animal in Africa is not the lion, it's the hippopotamus.
Cel mai periculos animal din Africa nu este leul, ci hipopotamul.
A wolf is much bigger than a fox.
Un lup este mult mai mare decât o vulpe.
Are there bears in this forest?
Există urşi în această pădure?
Bats are the only mammals that can fly.
Liliecii sunt singurele mamifere care pot zbura.
It's usually very difficult to see a leopard in the wild.
De obicei, este foarte dificil să vezi un leopard în sălbăticie.
Cheetahs are common in certain regions of Africa and rare in others.
Gheparzii sunt obişnuiţi în anumite regiuni din Africa şi rari în altele.
Elephants and rhinoceroses are known as very aggressive animals.
Elefanţii şi rinocerii sunt cunoscuţi ca animale foarte agresive.
I saw a hyena and a panther at the safari yesterday.
Am văzut o hienă şi o panteră la safari ieri.
The largest member of the cat family is the tiger.
Cel mai mare membru al familiei de pisici este tigrul.
Deer hunting is forbidden in the national park.
Vânătoarea de căprioare este interzisă în parcul naţional.
There are many monkeys on the branches of the trees.
Pe ramurile copacilor sunt multe maimuţe.
An opossum isn't a rat but it's a marsupial just like the kangaroo.
Un opossum nu este un şobolan, dar este un marsupial la fel ca cangurul.

Bird - Pasăre
Crow - Corb
Stork - Barză
Vulture - Vultur/ **Eagle -** Acvilă
Owl - Bufniță
Peacock - Păun
Frog - Broască
Reptile - Reptilă
Turtle - Broască țestoasă
Snake - Șarpe/ **Lizard -** Șopârlă/ **Crocodile -** Crocodil
Seal - Focă / **Whale -** Balenă/ **Dolphin –** Delfin
Fish - Pește
Shark - Rechin
Wing - Aripă/ **Feather -** Pană
Tail - Coadă
Fur - Blană
Scales - Solzi
Fins - Aripioare
Horns - Coarne
Claws - Gheare

An eagle and an owl are birds of prey however vultures are scavengers.
Un vultur și o bufniță sunt păsări de pradă, dar vulturii sunt animale necrofage.
Crows are very smart.
Ciorile sunt foarte inteligente.
I want to see the stork migration in Europe.
Vreau să văd migrația berzei în Europa.
Don't buy a fur coat!
Nu cumpăra o haină de blană!
Butterflies and peacocks are colorful.
Fluturii și păunii sunt colorați.
Some snakes are poisonous.
Unii șerpi sunt otrăvitori.
Is that the sound of a cricket or a frog?
Acesta este sunetul unui greiere sau al unei broaște?
Lizards, crocodiles, and turtles belong to the reptile family.
Șopârlele, crocodilii și țestoasele aparțin familiei reptilelor.
I want to see the fish in the lake.
Vreau să văd peștii din lac.
There were a lot of seals basking on the beach last week.
Au fost o mulțime de foci pe plajă săptămâna trecută.
A whale is not a fish.
O balenă nu este un pește.

Insect - Insectă
A cricket - Un greiere
Ant - Furnică**/ Termite -** Termită
A fly - O muscă **/ Butterfly -** Fluture
Worm - Vierme
Mosquito – Ţânţar/ **Flea -** Purice**/ Lice -** Paduchi
Beetle - Cărăbuş
A roach - Un gândac
Bee - Albină
Spider - Păianjen**/ Scorpion -** Scorpion
Snail - Melc
Invertebrates - Nevertebrate
Shrimps - Creveți/ **Clams -** Scoici**/ Crab -** Crab
Octopus - Caracatiță
Starfish - Steaua de mare
Jellyfish - Meduză

An octopus has eight tentacles.
O caracatiță are opt tentacule.
A jellyfish is a common dish in Asian culture.
O meduză este un fel de mâncare comun în cultura asiatică.
The museum has a large collection of invertebrate fossils.
Muzeul are o mare colecție de fosile de nevertebrate.
I want to buy mosquito spray.
Vreau să cumpăr spray pentru ţânţari.
I need antiseptic for my bug bites.
Am nevoie de antiseptic pentru muşcăturile de insecte.
I hope there aren't any worms, ants, or flies in the bag of sugar.
Sper să nu fie viermi, furnici sau muşte în punga cu zahăr.
I have crabs and starfish in my aquarium.
Am crabi şi stele de mare în acvariul meu.
Certain types of spiders and scorpions can be dangerous.
Anumite tipuri de păianjeni şi scorpioni pot fi periculoase.
I need to call the exterminator because there are fleas, roaches, and termites in my house.
Trebuie să sun la deratizare pentru că în casa mea sunt purici, gândaci şi termite.
Bees are very important for the environment.
Albinele sunt foarte importante pentru mediu.
Is there a snail inside the shell?
Este un melc în interiorul cochiliei?
Beetles are my favorite insects.
Gândacii sunt insectele mele preferate.

RELIGION, CELEBRATIONS, & CUSTOMS
RELIGIE, SĂRBĂTORI ȘI OBICEIURI

God - Dumnezeu/ **Bible -** Biblie
Old Testament - Vechiul Testament **/ New Testament -** Noul Testament
Adam - Adam **/ Eve -** Eva **/ Noah -** Noe**/ Ark -** Arca
Garden of Eden - Grădina Edenului / **Heaven -** Rai
To pray - A se ruga **/ Prayer -** Rugăciunea**/ Holy -** Sfânt**/ Faith -** Credință
Blessing - Binecuvântare/ **To bless -** A binecuvânta
Moses - Moise**/ Prophet -** Profet**/ Messiah -** Mesia/ **Miracle -** Miracol
Ten commandments - Zece porunci
The five books of Moses - Cele cinci cărți ale lui Moise
Genesis - Geneza**/ Exodus -** Exod**/ Leviticus -** Leviticul
Numbers - Numere**/ Deuteronomy -** Deuteronom

What is your religion?
Care este religia ta?
Many religions use the bible.
Multe religii folosesc Biblia.
We have faith in miracles.
Avem încredere în miracole.
When do I need to say the blessing?
Când trebuie să spun rugăciunea de binecuvântare?
I must say a prayer for the holiday.
Trebuie să spun o rugăciune pentru sărbătoare.
The angels came from heaven.
Îngerii au venit din rai.
Aaron, the brother of Moses, was the first priest.
Aaron, fratele lui Moise, a fost primul preot.
The story of Noah's Ark and the flood is very interesting.
Povestea Arcei lui Noe și a potopului este foarte interesantă.
Adam and Eve were the first humans and they lived in the Garden of Eden.
Adam și Eva au fost primii oameni și au trăit în Grădina Edenului.
Moses had to climb up on Mount Sinai to receive the Ten Commandments from God.
Moise a trebuit să se urce pe Muntele Sinai pentru a primi cele Zece Porunci de la Dumnezeu.
The Five Books of the Moses are Genesis, Exodus, Leviticus, Numbers, and Deuteronomy.
Cele cinci cărți ale lui Moise sunt Geneza, Exodul, Leviticul, Numerele și Deuteronom.
Moses was considered as the prophet of all prophets.
Moise a fost considerat profetul tuturor profeților.

The Christian Religion - Religia creştină
Church - Biserică
Cathedral - Catedrală
Catholic - Catolic
Christian - Creştin / **Christianity -** Creştinism
Catholicism - Catolicism
Jesus - Isus
A cross - O cruce
Priest - Preot
Holy - Sfânt/ **Holy water -** Apă sfinţită
To sin - A păcătui/ **A sin -** Un păcat
Monastery - Manastire
Christmas - Crăciun
Christmas eve - Ajunul Crăciunului
Christmas tree - Brad de Crăciun
New Year - Anul Nou
Merry Christmas - Crăciun Fericit
Easter - Paşte
Saint - Sfânt/ **Nun -** Călugăriţă

The church is open today.
Biserica este deschisă astăzi.
Christians love to celebrate Christmas.
Creştinilor le place să sărbătorească Crăciunul.
Is it possible to turn on the lights on my Christmas tree for Christmas Eve?
Este posibil să aprind luminile bradului meu de Căciun în Ajunul Crăciunului?
Two more weeks until Easter.
Încă două săptămâni până la Paşti.
The nuns live in the monastery.
Călugăriţele locuiesc în mănăstire.
The priest read a psalm from the Bible in front of the congregation.
Preotul a citit un psalm din Biblie în faţa congregaţiei.
I went to pray in the cathedral.
M-am dus să mă rog în catedrală.
Happy holiday and Happy New Year to all my friends and family.
Sărbători fericite şi La Mulţi Ani tuturor prietenilor şi familiei mele.
The priest baptized the baby in the holy water.
Preotul a botezat pruncul în apă sfinţită.
The devil and the demons are from hell.
Diavolul şi demonii sunt din iad.
Many schools refuse to teach evolution.
Multe şcoli refuză să predea teoria evoluţiei.

Jew - Evreu
Judaism - Iudaism
Passover - Paşte
Kosher - Kosher
Circumcision - Circumcizie
Synagogue - Sinagogă
Goblet - Pahar
Wine - Vin
Religious - Religios
Monotheism - Monoteism
Islam - Islam
Muslim - Musulman
Mohammed - Mohammed
Mosque - Moschee
Hindu - Hindus
Buddhist - Budist
Temple - Templu

The Jews worship at the synagogue.
Evreii se închină la sinagogă.
The Bible is a holy book which tells the story of the Jewish nations and includes many miracles.
Biblia este o carte sfântă care spune povestea naţiunilor evreieşti şi include multe miracole.
In Judaism, they pray three times a day. Morning prayer, afternoon prayer, and evening prayer.
În iudaism, ei se roagă de trei ori pe zi. Rugăciunea de dimineaţă, rugăciunea de după-amiază şi rugăciunea de seară.
The three forefathers are Abraham, Isaac, and Jacob.
Cei trei prooroci sunt Avraam, Isaac şi Iacob.
To learn about the Holocaust and the concentration camps is very important.
Este foarte important să înveţi despre Holocaust şi despre lagărele de concentrare.
Both the Hindu and Buddhist religion practice yoga, meditation and mantra.
Atât religia hindusă, cât şi cea budistă practică yoga, meditaţia şi mantra.
Muslims worship at the mosque.
Musulmanii se închină la moschee.
In Islam you must pray five times a day.
În islam trebuie să te rogi de cinci ori pe zi.

WEDDING AND RELATIONSHIP NUNTĂ ŞI RELAŢIE

Wedding - Nuntă
Wedding hall - Sala de nunţi
Married - Căsătorit
Civil wedding - Cununie civilă
Bride - Mireasă
Groom - Mire
Ceremony - Ceremonie
Reception hall - Sală de recepţie
Chapel - Capelă
Engagement - Logodnă
Engagement ring - Inel de logodnă
Wedding ring - Verighetă
Anniversary - Aniversare
Honeymoon - Lună de miere
Fiancé - Logodnic
Husband - Soț
Wife - Nevastă
Invitations - Invitații
To invite - A invita

When is the wedding?
Cand este nunta?
We are having the service in the chapel and the reception in the wedding hall.
Slujba va avea loc în capelă, iar recepţia în sala de nunţi.
This is my engagement ring and this is my wedding ring.
Acesta este inelul meu de logodnă şi acesta este verigheta mea.
He is my fiancé now. Next year he will be my husband.
El este logodnicul meu acum. Anul viitor va fi soțul meu.
They are finally married so now it's time for the honeymoon.
În sfârşit sunt căsătoriţi, aşa că acum este timpul pentru luna de miere.
He decided to propose to his girlfriend. She said "yes" and now they are engaged.
A decis să-și ceară în căsătorie iubita. Ea a spus „da" și acum s-au logodit.
I must/need to send the wedding invitations.
Trebuie să trimit invitațiile de nuntă.
Three civil weddings are taking place at the courthouse today.
Trei cununii civile au loc astăzi la tribunal.
The bride and groom received many presents.
Mirii au primit multe cadouri.
Our anniversary is on Valentine's Day.
Aniversarea noastră este de Ziua Îndrăgostiților.

Valentine day - Ziua Îndrăgostiţilor
Love - Dragoste
To love - A iubi
In love - Îndrăgostit
Romantic - Romantic
Darling - Dragă
A date - O întâlnire
A relationship - O relaţie
Boyfriend - Iubit
Girlfriend - Iubită
To hug - A îmbrăţişa
A hug - O îmbrăţişare
To kiss - A săruta
A kiss - Un sărut
Single - Singur
Divorced - Divorţat
Widow - Văduvă

I am in love with her.
Sunt îndrăgostit de ea.
I love her.
O iubesc.
I love him.
Îl iubesc.
I love you.
Te iubesc.
You are very romantic.
Eşti foarte romantic.
They have a very good relationship.
Au o relaţie foarte bună.
The husband and wife are happily married.
Soțul și soția au o căsnicie fericită.
I am single because I divorced my wife.
Sunt singur pentru că am divorţat de soţia mea.
She is my darling and my love.
Ea este iubita şi dragostea mea.
I want to kiss you and hug you in this picture.
Vreau să te sărut și să te îmbrăţişez în această poză.
The widow still lives in the same house.
Văduva locuieşte încă în aceeaşi casă.
My boyfriend (also male friend) lives in Iaşi.
Prietenul meu locuieşte în Iaşi.

POLITICS - POLITICĂ

Flag - Steag
National anthem - Imn naţional
Nation - Naţiune
National – Naţional
International - Internaţional
Local - Local
Patriot - Patriot
Symbol - Simbol
Peace - Pace
Treaty - Tratat
State - Stat
Country - Ţară
County - Judeţ
Century - Secol
Legal - Legal
Sanctions - Sancţiuni
Riots - Revoltă
Riots - Răscoală
Protests - Proteste

This is a political movement which is supported by the majority.
Aceasta este o mişcare politică susţinută de majoritate.
This flag is the national symbol of the country.
Acest steag este simbolul naţional al ţării.
This is all politics.
Este vorba doar de politică.
There is a difference between state law and local law.
Există o diferenţă între legislaţia naţională şi cea locală.
He is a patriot of the nation.
El este un patriot al naţiunii.
Most countries have a national anthem.
Majoritatea ţărilor au un imn naţional.
This is a political campaign to demand independence.
Aceasta este o campanie politică pentru a cere independenţa.
In which county is this legal?
In ce judet este legal acest lucru?
They must impose sanctions against that country.
Ei trebuie să impună sancţiuni împotriva acelei ţări.
There were many protests and riots today.
Au fost multe proteste şi revolte astăzi.

Law - Lege
International law - Drept internaţional
Human rights - Drepturile omului
Punishment - Pedeapsă
Torture - Tortură
Execution (to kill) **–** Execuţie (a ucide)
Spy - Spion
Amnesty - Amnistie
Political asylum - Azil politic
Republic - Republică
Dictator - Dictator
Citizen - Cetăţean
Resident - Rezident
Immigrant - Imigrant
Public - Public
Private - Privat
Racism - Rasism
Government - Guvern
Revolution - Revoluție
Civilian - Civil
A civilian - Un civil
Population - Populație
Socialism - Socialism
Communism - Comunism

The civilian population wanted a revolution.
Populația civilă a dorit o revoluție.
The politicians want to ask the president to give the captured spy amnesty.
Politicienii vor să-i ceară preşedintelui să acorde amnistia spionului capturat.
Although he was the brutal dictator of the republic, in private he was a nice person.
Deși era dictatorul brutal al republicii, în privat era o persoană agreabilă.
In some countries torture and execution is a common form of legitimate punishment.
În unele ţări, tortura și execuţia sunt o formă comună de pedeapsă legală.
This is a violation of human rights and international law.
Aceasta este o încălcare a drepturilor omului și a dreptului internațional.
Communism and socialism were popular in the 19th century.
Comunismul și socialismul au fost populare în secolul al XIX-lea.

President - Preşedinte
Statement - Declaraţie
Presidential - Prezidenţial
Vice president - Vicepreşedinte
Defense minister - Ministrul Apărării
Interior minister - Ministrul de Interne
Exterior minister - Ministrul de Externe
Prime minister - Prim-ministru
Election - Alegere
Poll - Sondaj
Campaign - Campanie
Candidate - Candidat
Democracy - Democraţie
Movement - Mişcare
Politician - Politician
Politics - Politică
To vote - A vota
Majority - Majoritate
Independence - Independenţă
Party - Partid
Veto - Veto
Impeachment - Punerea sub acuzare
Convoy - Convoi
Illegal - Ilegal

They want to appoint him as defense minister.
Vor să-l numească ministru al apărării.
Both parties want to veto the impeachment inquiry.
Ambele partide vor să se opună prin veto la ancheta de destituire..
I want to see the presidential convoy.
Vreau să văd convoiul prezidenţial.
In some countries other than the United States, they have a prime minister, interior minister, and exterior minister.
În unele ţări, altele decât Statele Unite, au un prim-ministru, un ministru de interne şi un ministru de externe.
I want to meet the president and the vice president.
Vreau să mă întâlnesc cu preşedintele şi vicepreşedintele.
I want to go to the election polls to vote for the new candidate.
Vreau să merg la urne pentru a vota noul candidat.
We support democracy and are against fascism and racism.
Susţinem democraţia şi suntem împotriva fascismului şi rasismului.

United Nations - Naţiuni Unite
Condemnation - Condamnare
United States - Statele Unite ale Americii
European Union - Uniunea Europeană
Military coup - Lovitură de stat militară
Treason - Trădare
Fascism - Fascism
Resistance - Rezistenţă
Members - Membri
Captured - Capturat
To capture - A captura
Ambassador - Ambasador
Embassy - Ambasadă
Consulate - Consulat
Biased - Părtinitor
Unilateral - Unilateral
Bilateral - Bilateral
Resolution - Rezoluţie
Rebels - Rebeli

All the members of the resistance were accused of treason and had to ask for political asylum.
Toţi membrii rezistenţei au fost acuzaţi de trădare şi au fost nevoiţi să ceară azil politic.
The resolution is biased.
Soluţia este părtinitoare.
This was an official condemnation.
Aceasta a fost o condamnare oficială.
The United Nations is located in New York.
Organizaţia Naţiunilor Unite este situată la New York.
I am a United States citizen and a resident of the European Union.
Sunt cetăţean al Statelor Unite şi rezident al Uniunii Europene.
The ambassador's residence is located near the embassy.
Reşedinţa ambasadorului este situată în apropierea ambasadei.
I need the phone number and address of the consulate.
Am nevoie de numărul de telefon şi adresa consulatului.
Are consular services available today?
Serviciile consulare sunt disponibile astăzi?
The international peace treaty needs to include both sides.
Tratatul internaţional de pace trebuie să includă ambele părţi.
According to the government, the rebels carried out an illegal military coup.
Potrivit guvernului, rebelii au dat o lovitură militară de stat ilegală.

MILITARY - MILITAR

Army - Armată
Armed forces - Forțele armate
Navy - Marină
Soldier - Soldat
A force - O forță
Ground forces - Forțe terestre
War - Război
Base - Bază/ **Headquarter –** Cartier general
Intelligence – Serviciu de informații
Ranks - Rânduri/ **Sergeant** - Sergent/ **Lieutenant** - Locotenent
The general - Generalul**/ Commander** - Comandant**/ Colonel** - Colonel
Chief of Staff - Șeful Statului Major
Enlistment - Înrolare **/ Reserves** - Rezerve
Terrorism - Terorism**/ Terrorist** - Terorist**/ Insurgency** - Insurecție
Border crossing - Trecerea frontierei
Refugee - Refugiat **/ Camp** - Cantonament

I want to enlist in the military.
Vreau să mă înrolez în armată.
This base is designated for military aircraft only.
Această bază este destinată numai aeronavelor militare.
That is the headquarters of the enemy.
Acesta este cartierul general al inamicului.
This country has a powerful airforce.
Această țară are o forță aeriană puternică.
They need to enlist reserve forces for the war.
Ei trebuie să înroleze forțe de rezervă pentru război.
Welcome to the border crossing.
Bun venit la punctul de trecere a frontierei.
Military intelligence relies on important sources of information.
Informațiile militare se bazează pe surse importante de informații.
The chief of staff was the target of a failed assassination attempt.
Șeful de stat major a fost ținta unei tentative de asasinat eșuate.
The sniper killed the highest-ranking lieutenant.
Lunetistul l-a ucis pe locotenentul cu cel mai înalt rang.
The terrorist group claimed responsibility for the car-bomb attack at the refugee camp.
Gruparea teroristă a revendicat atacul cu mașină-bombă din tabăra de refugiați.
It is impossible to defeat terrorism because it's an ideology.
Este imposibil să învingi terorismul pentru că este o ideologie.

Air force - Forţele aeriene/ **Fighter jet -** Avion de luptă
Air strike - Lovitură aeriană / **Military aircraft -** Avion militar
Drone - Dronă/ **Stealth technology -** Tehnologia Camuflaj
Tank - Tanc/ **Submarine -** Submarin
Weapon - Armă / **Ammunition -** Muniţie
Grenade - Grenadă/ **Mine -** Mină/ **Bomb -** Bombă/ **Explosion -** Explozie
Sniper - Lunetist/ **Gun -** Armă/ **Rifle -** Puşcă/ **Bullet -** Glonţ
Missile - Rachetă/ **Mortar -** Mortar
Anti tank missile - Rachetă antitanc
Anti aircraft missile - Rachetă antiaeriană
Shoulder fire missile – Lansator de rachete mobil
Artillery - Artilerie/ **Artillery shell -** Obuz de artilerie
Precision missile - Rachetă de precizie/ **Ballistic missile -** Rachetă balistică
Atomic bomb - Bombă atomică / **Nuclear weapon -** Armă nucleară
Weapon of mass destruction - Armă de distrugere în masă
Chemical weapon - Armă chimică
Flare system - Sistem de semnalizare
Supply - Aprovizionare/ **Storage -** Depozitare / **Armor -** Armură

The M-16 is a US-made rifle.
M-16 este o mitralieră fabricată în SUA.
The tank fired artillery shells.
Tancul a tras cu obuze de artilerie.
Shoulder-fired missiles are extremely dangerous and are hard to defend against.
Rachetele lansate de la umăr sunt extrem de periculoase şi sunt greu de evitat.
The flare system is meant as a defense against anti-aircraft missiles.
Sistemul de rachete de balizaj este destinat apărării împotriva rachetelor antiaeriene.
The navy was able to intercept a missile.
Marina a reuşit să intercepteze o rachetă.
At the terrorist safe-house, guns, bullets, and grenades were found.
La refugiul terorist au fost găsite arme, gloanţe şi grenade.
The coalition forces struck an enemy arms depot.
Forţele coaliţiei au lovit un depozit de arme inamice.
An intense missile attack was carried out against the supply forces that resulted in many casualties.
Un atac intens cu rachete a fost efectuat împotriva forţelor de aprovizionare, care s-a soldat cu multe victime.
The terrorist cell fired ballistic missiles at the nuclear facility site.
Celula teroristă a tras rachete balistice spre amplasamentul instalaţiei nucleare.
Atomic bombs and chemical weapons are weapons of mass destruction.
Bombele atomice şi armele chimice sunt arme de distrugere în masă.

A target - O țintă / **To target** - A ținti
An attack - Un atac / **To attack** - A ataca / **Intense** - Intens
To shoot - A trage / **Open fire** - Foc deschis/ **Fired** - Tras
Enemy - Inamic **/ Assassination** - Asasinat**/ Assassin** - Asasin
Reconnaissance - Recunoaștere
To infiltrate - A se infiltra/ **Invasion** - Invazie
Exchange of fire - Schimb de foc
A cease fire – Un acord de încetare a focului **/ Withdrawal** - Retragere
To win - A câștiga / **To surrender** - A se preda
Victim - Victimă/ **Injured** - Accidentat**/ Wounded** - Rănit
Deaths - Decese**/ Killed** - Ucis/ **To kill** - A ucide
Prisoner of war - Prizonier de război
Missing in action - Dispărut în acțiune
Act of war - Act de război / **War crimes** - Crime de război
Defense - Apărare **/ Attempt** - Încercare

There is an invasion of ground forces.
Există o invazie a forțelor terestre.
The soldier wanted to open fire and shoot at the invading forces.
Soldatul a vrut să deschidă focul și să tragă în forțele invadatoare.
The bomb attack was considered an act of aggression and an act of war.
Atacul cu bombă a fost considerat un act de agresiune și un act de război.
The reconnaissance drone managed to infiltrate deep within enemy territory.
Drona de recunoaștere a reușit să se infiltreze adânc în teritoriul inamic.
The airstrike targeted an ammunition storage site.
Atacul aerian a vizat un loc de depozitare a muniției.
The mortar attack and exchange of fire caused injuries and deaths on both sides.
Atacul cu mortar și schimbul de foc au provocat răni și morți de ambele părți.
First, we need to clear the mines.
În primul rând, trebuie să curățăm terenul de mine.
The ceasefire agreement included the release of prisoners of war.
Acordul de încetare a focului a inclus eliberarea prizonierilor de război.
The army made a public statement to announce the withdrawal.
Armata a făcut o declarație publică pentru a anunța retragerea.
There was a huge explosion as a result of the terrorist attack.
A avut loc o explozie uriașă în urma atacului terorist.
The commander of the insurgency was accused of serious war crimes.
Comandantul insurgenților a fost acuzat de grave crime de război.
Several of the submarine sailors were missing in action.
Mai mulți marinari ai submarinului au fost dați dispăruți în misiune.

Conclusion

Hopefully, you have enjoyed this book and will use the knowledge you have learned in various situations in your everyday life. In contrast to other methods of learning foreign languages, the theory in this current usage is that ever-greater topics can be broached so that one's vocabulary can expand. This method relies on the discovery I made of the list of core words from each language. Once these are learned, your conversational learning skills will progress very quickly.

You are now ready to discuss sport and school and office-related topics and this will open up your world to a more satisfying extent. Humans are social creatures and language helps us interact. Indeed, at times, it can keep us alive, such as in war situations. You might find yourself in dangerous situations perhaps as a journalist, military personnel or civilian and you need to be armed with the appropriate vocabulary.

"This is a base for military aircraft only," you may have to tell some people who try to enter a field you are protecting, or know what you are being told when someone says to you, "Welcome to the border crossing." As a journalist on a foreign assignment, you may need to quickly understand what you are being told, such as "The sniper killed the highest-ranking lieutenant." If you are someone negotiating on behalf of the army, you may need to find another lieutenant very quickly. Lives, at times, literally depend on your level of understanding and comprehension.

This unique approach that I first discovered when using this method to learn on my own, will have helped you speak the Romanian language much quicker than any other way.

Congratulations! Now You Are on Your Own!

If you merely absorb the required words in this book, you will then have acquired the basis to become conversational in Romanian! After memorizing these words, this conversational foundational basis that you have just gained will trigger your ability to make improvements in conversational fluency at an amazing speed! However, in order to engage in quick and easy conversational communication, you need a special type of basics, and this book will provide you with just that.

Unlike the foreign language learning systems presently used in schools and universities, along with books and programs that are available on the market today, that focus on *everything* but being conversational, *this* method's sole focus is on becoming conversational in Romanian as well as any other language. Once you have successfully mastered the required words in this book, there are two techniques that if combined with these essential words, can further enhance your skills and will result in you improving your proficiency tenfold. *However*, these two techniques will only succeed *if* you have completely and successfully absorbed these required words. *After* you establish the basis for fluent communications by memorizing these words, you can enhance your conversational abilities even more if you use the following two techniques.

The first step is to attend a Romanian language class that will enable you to sharpen your grammar. You will gain additional vocabulary and learn past and present tenses, and if you apply these skills that you learn in the class, together with these words that you have previously memorized, you will be improving your conversational skills tenfold. You will notice that, conversationally, you will succeed at a much higher rate than any of your classmates. A simple second technique is to choose Romanian subtitles while watching a movie. If you have successfully mastered and grasped these words, then the combination of the two—those words along with the subtitles—will aid you considerably in putting all the grammar into perspective, and again, conversationally, you will improve tenfold.

Once you have established a basis of quick and easy conversation in Romanian with those words that you just attained, every additional word or grammar rule you pick up from there on will be gravy. And these additional words or grammar rules can be combined with the these words, enriching your conversational abilities even more. Basically, after the research and studies I've conducted with my method over the years, I came to the conclusion that in order to become conversational, you first must learn the words and *then* learn the grammar.

The Romanian language is compatible with the mirror translation technique. Likewise, with *this* language, you can use this mirror translation technique in order to become conversational, enabling you to communicate even more effortlessly. Mirror translation is the method of translating a phrase or sentence, word for word from English to Romanian, by using these imperative words that you have acquired through this program (such as the sentences I used in this book). Latin languages, Middle Eastern languages, and Slavic languages, along with a few others, are also compatible with the mirror translation technique. Though you won't be speaking perfectly proper and precise Romanian, you will still be fully understood and, conversation-wise, be able to get by just fine.

NOTE FROM THE AUTHOR

Thank you for your interest in my work. I encourage you to share your overall experience of this book by posting a review. Your review can make a difference! Please feel free to describe how you benefited from my method or provide creative feedback on how I can improve this program. I am constantly seeking ways to enhance the quality of this product, based on personal testimonials and suggestions from individuals like you. In order to post a review, please check with the retailer of this book.

Thanks and best of luck,
Yatir Nitzany

Also by Yatir Nitzany

Conversational Spanish Quick and Easy

....

Conversational French Quick and Easy

....

Conversational Italian Quick and Easy

....

Conversational Portuguese Quick and Easy

....

Conversational Romanian Quick and Easy

....

Conversational German Quick and Easy

....

Conversational Dutch Quick and Easy

....

Conversational Norwegian Quick and Easy

....

Conversational Danish Quick and Easy

....

Conversational Swedish Quick and Easy

....

Conversational Finnish Quick and Easy

....

Conversational Russian Quick and Easy

....

Conversational Ukrainian Quick and Easy

....

Conversational Bulgarian Quick and Easy

....

Conversational Polish Quick and Easy

....

Conversational Hebrew Quick and Easy

....

Conversational Yiddish Quick and Easy

....

Conversational Armenian Quick and Easy

....

Conversational Arabic Quick and Easy

....

www.ingramcontent.com/pod-product-compliance
Ingram Content Group UK Ltd.
Pitfield, Milton Keynes, MK11 3LW, UK
UKHW020423250726
13967UKWH00007B/2785